A Mother's Story

A Mother's Story

✦

Memories from the Turtle Creek Valley

Maryann B. Lawrence

iUniverse, Inc.
New York   Bloomington

A Mother's Story
Memories from the Turtle Creek Valley

The views expressed in this work are solely those of the author and do not necessarily reflect the views of the publisher, and the publisher hereby disclaims any responsibility for them.

iUniverse books may be ordered through booksellers or by contacting:

iUniverse
1663 Liberty Drive
Bloomington, IN 47403
www.iuniverse.com
1-800-Authors (1-800-288-4677)

Because of the dynamic nature of the Internet, any Web addresses or links contained in this book may have changed since publication and may no longer be valid.

ISBN: 978-1-4502-1430-8 (sc)
ISBN: 978-1-4502-1433-9 (dj)
ISBN: 978-1-4502-1432-2 (ebk)

Library of Congress Control Number: 2010902905

Printed in the United States of America
s
iUniverse rev. date: 3/18/2010

Dedication

*This book is dedicated to my family, my children,
and my grandchildren.
Always remember who you are and where you came from.*

*With My Love,
Mom*

Table of Contents

About the Author

Born on the second day of December in 1925, Maryann B. Lawrence is the second daughter of Joseph Krzyzosiak and Helen (Figulski) Krzyzosiak. Along with Irene, her older sister, Maryann enjoyed a wonderful childhood full of fun and adventure on the hill known as Electric Plan, in the little town of Turtle Creek in southwestern Pennsylvania

There Maryann was surrounded by the love of her parents, grandparents, and extended family that lived close by. With the hard work and ingenuity of her father, and the convictions and passion of her mother, they survived the Great Depression. She was taught the importance of strong family values of honesty, fairness and good character, and preserving the rich customs of her Polish-German heritage.

While attending Turtle Creek Union High School, she met and married Walter Lawrence, during the turbulent times of World War II. Just as her parents had done before her, they settled on the hill known as Electric Plan and started a family. Along with her husband, she enjoyed her young adulthood with her children and instilled in them the same character and values that make her the person that she is today.

After attending business school, Maryann enjoyed a twenty-eight year career in retail sales and management with a major department store. Best of all, Maryann was a loving wife to Walter, and is a loving mother, and grandmother. She is a cherished true friend and neighbor to many. An avid reader, she enjoys a good book. She appreciates good music, and stimulating conversation.

Maryann enjoyed living in Turtle Creek for over sixty years. After retirement she moved to the desert southwest with Walter. She now enjoys living with her children, grandchildren, and Maggie, her Scottish terrier, in sunny Las Vegas, Nevada.

While working on a project for her family and children, Maryann discovered her gifted talent as a writer. Meant to document family history and tell the story of her life, that project has blossomed into this wonderful book. It clearly reflects her voice, her charm, and her wit. This has been a creative and positive endeavor for her, taking her life in a different direction and giving it new meaning and purpose. After all, everyone has a history and a story to tell.

Introduction

Boredom....does it come with age or is it simply in the imagination? Hopefully, it isn't a form of senility. Here I am in my eighth decade and I'm bored stiff. That is my problem exactly. Everyone is at work all day and here I sit with our Scottish terrier. There is music which has always been the background to my day. I've read many books and have done many crocheting projects but now, I need another purpose. I am not one to just sit idle and watch the years keep going by. The television programs of today leave me cold and not entertained. I must find something constructive to do. Something exciting and something positive is needed to occupy my time and my mind. Throughout the day, memories come flooding back and capture me for a moment or two. These memories invigorate me and bring feelings of warmth and comfort.

On numerous occasions, I have been asked to provide information pertaining to past events and family history. "Who's that in the old photograph?" or "Do you remember when...?" This is part of the honor bestowed upon some of the eldest of family members. I'm fortunate enough to have a clear recollection of what was told to me by my parents and grandparents, many years ago and to be able to provide the information.

It has always been suggested that I write down everything I remember. Inspiring me, were my children and a cousin, who acts as the family historian. Perhaps, this wasn't such a bad idea after all. I got my first composition book at the grocery store, one Friday evening. The next Monday, once everyone left to start their day, I sat at the table in our sunny breakfast area and began to write. It became almost hypnotic, as the more I wrote, the more I remembered. It was amazing how easily the memories came back to me. This endeavor was becoming a gift as I was truly enjoying the task. The heat of the summer was beginning to fade into fall and I was still writing. Each day, I would visit with my memories and record them in my composition books. My routine continued on throughout the next, complete year. This was becoming an incredible tribute to my family, my heritage, and to life as I knew it in Turtle Creek, a small town in western Pennsylvania.

Once inhabited by a small tribe of the Delaware Indians, the Turtle Creek Valley is rich in a history all of its own. It grew from a small settlement around a stagecoach stop, to a bustling, thriving community. The town of

Turtle Creek was located between two small companies that were founded by George Westinghouse, one of the entrepreneurs of the industrial revolution. One of the first radio broadcasts originated at the Westinghouse Electric Company from the top of the "K" building, in November 1920, to announce the election victory of Warren G. Harding.

Surrounding Turtle Creek Valley were beautiful hills, covered with dense woods. My mother's family was among the first residents to settle on one of the hills that overlooked the valley. The hill was known as Electric Plan. This idyllic setting was the perfect place to settle and raise a family. This is where the magic of my life began. My family contributed to the rich history of Turtle Creek for three generations.

Preserving history is very valuable and important to future generations. History is the foundation to everything and everyone. My ancestors originated in Eastern Europe, in areas of Germany and Poland. My grandparents were part of the huge influx of immigrants who came to America in the mid to late 1800s. They settled in western Pennsylvania. Their lives were very difficult. They faced many hardships as they assimilated into American culture and became productive members of society. My grandparents worked very hard to provide a better life for themselves and their children. And they were so proud to become American citizens.

Telling one's own story is equally important. Often, I would quietly observe as our children would climb into my parent's lap and say, "Please tell me about when..." I would listen as they would become completely enthralled by the same stories that were told to my sister and me when we were children. These were not tall tales, but actual events that occurred in the lives of my parents and grandparents. My mother would relate tales of her early childhood in a rural mining town. My father would tell of his struggles as an orphan and of his adventures in the Navy. They would speak about the trying times of the Great Depression and how they survived.

I want to share and preserve my life experiences not only for my family, but for those that share an interest in similar backgrounds. Life in a small town can be a wonderful experience that many will never know. It could have just simply been the time and the place, but it was almost magical. Even though my life may seem quite ordinary to some, to me, it was a happy, exciting adventure.

It worries me that the family structure of today has changed. Values seem skewed and are completely different. Most people tend to be so self-absorbed. The precious time that was once spent with parents and grandparents is now substituted with devices of modern technology. Many lives lack the human experience and the human touch, not just physically, but emotionally and spiritually. The interest in the past is just not there and the respect for the past is gone. Life is like a beautiful tapestry. Our history makes up the background. Our character creates the pattern. Our heritage makes the weave of the fabric strong. The memories and the events in our lives are the beautiful, colorful threads that give it life.

My journey will take you back to when times and life in general, were much more simple and enjoyable. These times and places will never exist as they once were, and that is what makes my story and my life unique. The path that we choose and the direction we take, determine the outcome and the degree of contentment we achieve in life. The insignificant experiences that we have along the way add flavor, shape our personality, and leave imprints on our souls. Perhaps, these are the experiences that help to make us who we really are. This is my story and my legacy to my family and to all who read it.

My Father, Joseph Krzyzosiak and His Family

My father, Joseph Krzyzosiak, was born in Braddock, Pennsylvania on May 17, 1895. Braddock was a small town along the banks of the Monongahela River built around the Edgar Thompson Steel Mill, east of Pittsburgh. Before the mill, it was a small settlement known as Braddock's Field.

My father's parents, Andrew and Barbara Krzyzosiak came to the United States from Germany to make a new life and raise a family. Andrew was 34 years old when he arrived in New York, on May 9, 1884, on the ship *S.S. America*. Barbara, along with their three young daughters, Anna, Franzisca, and Victoria, arrived in New York on June 29, 1885, on the ship *S.S. Elbe*. She was 32 years old at that time. Her maiden name was Emilie Bertha Sonnenberger, but was changed to Sonnenberg. Her first name was later changed to Barbara, which is my middle name.

Andrew and Barbara first settled in a little town called Steelton, Pennsylvania, near where his brothers, Kajitan, Matthew, and Anthony, who had immigrated earlier, had settled. Steelton was located near Harrisburg, along the banks of the Susquehanna River. While living there, they had four more children, Max, Helena, Cecilia, and Valentina (Stacia). By 1892, the family moved to Braddock where three more children were born, John, Joseph (my father), and Edward. They lived on Halket and Seventh Streets, at Number Three, Bruggeman's Row. Census records show Andrew worked for Joseph Bruggemann in real estate in some capacity in the early 1900s. He also worked in the Edgar Thompson Steel Mill, which was owned by a prominent industrialist family in Pittsburgh.

My father always spoke of the great hardships and the poor living conditions experienced during his early years. Bruggemann's Row was along one of the spurs of the railroad tracks that went into the steel mill and Pittsburgh from the outlying valleys beyond Braddock. He remembered when the trains would pass on the way to and from Pittsburgh; sometimes the conductors would throw packages of left-over food to the people along the tracks. He also remembered that once, in the middle of the night, his father took him to watch the cattle cars coming in on the tracks into the mill. A labor dispute was occurring at the time at the steel mill. My father was very young and didn't understand what was happening. The owner of the mill was bringing in people from the south to work in the mill and to stop the dispute.

Life was not easy for the immigrants. The jobs were very hard and dangerous. The hours were long and the wages were very low. It was quite a struggle to survive. The immigrants were hard workers and strong people with good work ethics. It was a time in which the good jobs were acquired by favors or a word from a relative. Most jobs were patterned by ethnicity and race. It was a very prejudiced system. The supervisors were English and Scottish men. Polish and Slavic men worked the open hearth furnaces. Serbian and Italian men worked the blast furnaces. Black men from the south did the unskilled labor.

The immigrants preserved their proud heritage by creating ethnic-based social organizations in which they would have frequent programs and events. These same immigrants would learn to speak English fluently, fly the American flag proudly, and strive to become productive American citizens. They were the backbone of the steel corporation and many other corporations in this country and were responsible for their growth and prosperity.

John, Stacia, and my father Joseph Krzyzosiak,
with their mother Barbara in 1900.

Braddock was a busy, thriving town in those days. Besides the steel mill, there were other small factories and many businesses. Shops that featured all of the finery and stylish clothing of the day lined the main street. My father was very young when he started doing small chores for Mr. Ohringer, the owner of a furniture store on Braddock Avenue. Mr. Ohringer was a very nice man and immediately took a liking to my father. When my father was about eight years old, he so desperately wanted to get his mother a set of china dishes that he had seen in the store. He took the dishes home to his mother one day, without telling Mr. Ohringer. He was planning on paying for them, once he had saved the money. One day, Mr. Ohringer came to visit, only to discover that my father's mother had a beautiful set of china dishes that had once been in his store. She showed them off proudly, telling him that Joseph had bought the dishes for her as a gift. Much to my father's surprise, Mr. Ohringer said nothing about the dishes. Very sheepishly, my father went to do more chores at the store the next day. Mr. Ohringer quietly told him that he could work off the cost of the dishes, and if he wanted anything else, to please let him know first.

Creating mischief is part of being a young boy. My father's brother, John, was no stranger to mischief. Pedestrians would stroll up and down Library Street from the Post Office and there were fine, large Victorian homes further up on the hill. On Library Street, near the Carnegie Library, there was a man who sold roasted peanuts from a cart. The street, which was made of cobblestone, was quite steep. So he would carefully position his cart by blocking one of the wheels with a rock. The peanut vendor had a small capuchin monkey and a hand-crank organ. As he would play the crank organ, the little monkey would dance. John was always quite amused by the monkey. One day, he was watching the monkey and teasingly making faces at him. The peanut vendor was getting angry and started scolding him. All of a sudden, John kicked the rock from under the wheel of the peanut cart and it started careening down the steep cobblestones of Library Street, where it crashed at the bottom of the hill.

My father's mother, Barbara had become ill and suffered from depression. She took her own life at the age of fifty-two, by drinking carbolic acid. She died on July 4, 1905 and was buried the next day in the old part of Braddock Cemetery, known as Monongahela Cemetery. The manner of her death was kept quiet by Andrew and the others, to protect the younger children.

My father was only ten years old when his mother died so tragically and it affected him and his siblings deeply. Life without their mother was even worse than it had been before. She used to play a zither and sing to them. All of the children missed her greatly. Andrew and the younger children moved to a boarding house on Washington Street. There was no supervision and my father began to rebel. He did not like to go to Sacred Heart School and often refused to go. He would play along the river, walking to where it met Turtle

Creek, at Port Perry, to catch turtles or go fishing. Many days, my father could be found swimming in the river or floating on logs. The nuns and the priest at Sacred Heart School were very upset with him. They would send his sister, Stacia, to find him. His mother was no longer there to protect him or come to his aid. He completed the third grade and did not go back to school.

In 1908, while living at 878 Willow Way, Andrew put on a new pair of shoes with slippery leather soles. He slipped at the top of the carpeted stairs and fell. After lying in an unconscious state, he died a few days later on November 13, of a cerebral hemorrhage. Andrew was buried on November 15, in the Monongahela Cemetery. As we were growing up, my father was so frightened that any of us would suffer the same fate as Andrew, he would take our new shoes and scuff the soles on the cement so they would no longer be slippery. My father did the same with the new shoes of his grandchildren.

After Andrew died, my father and his brother, John were left to struggle on their own. They would occasionally go to one of their sisters' homes. By that time, most of them were married. They were busy having babies and doing housekeeping which was no easy task in those days. My father felt so unwanted and alone. He survived the best way he could, but it was not easy. Mr. Ohringer took pity on my father and always found odd jobs for him to do. Mr. Ohringer paid my father to help take care of his horses and fine carriage at the livery stable in Braddock. The job helped keep him out of the weather and gave him money for food. The owner of Nil's Bakery shop would let my father sleep in the back room of one of the bakeries if he would help light the large ovens each morning. They would also leave him bread and occasional goodies to eat at night and something to drink.

John, who was three years older than my father, decided to join the Navy. He really enjoyed being in the Navy. John told Joseph what a good life it was and suggested that he do the same. My father decided that he would lie about his age and try to enlist. However, he was sent away because he was under the weight requirement. Disappointed by this, he told his friend, Mr. Ohringer, who gave him twenty-five cents to buy five pounds of bananas. Mr. Ohringer instructed Joseph to eat all of the bananas and then go back to the recruiting office. He passed the weight requirement and officially joined the Navy on September 29, 1910.

Joseph, not only enjoyed his life in the Navy, he loved it. He served his country proudly on many ships, including the S.S. *New Jersey, the S.S. Tennessee,* and the *S.S. Virginia.* Occasionally, he would see his brother, John, whose ship happened to be in the same port. It was such a nice coincidence to be able to visit with each other. Once, while docked in the New York harbor, my father and his sailor buddies went to see the great Houdini. It was the thrill of a lifetime and he talked about it often for the rest of his life. He always told the kids about it and what a real treat it was for him. As a Navy man, of course, he was tattooed. He had a large eagle on his chest. He had his parents' initials with a small heart between them tattooed on one arm. On his other arm, he had a hula dancer that would dance when he would flex his muscles. The kids loved it!

My father made many friends in the Navy, but his best lifelong friend was Joseph O'Brien. Joseph O'Brien and his wife, Mary (Mayme) were from Philadelphia. We affectionately called them, "Uncle Joe and Aunt Mayme." They truly were an aunt and uncle to us and our children until their deaths. They never had children and were very much a part of the family. Unfortunately, my father received a medical discharge from the Navy on February 3, 1917 because he was involved in a scalding accident aboard ship.

He appreciated his Navy friends. He valued the Navy for what it did for him and for everything he learned while enlisted. If my father had not been hurt, I'm certain he would have been a career Navy man. His brother, John retired from the Navy with over thirty years of service.

Joseph Krzyzosiak, while in the Navy, in 1916.

My father returned to Braddock, Pennsylvania. In 1918, he married Anna Spernak. One year later, she gave birth to a son whom they named Albert. This was during the influenza epidemic of 1918-1919. Anna died a few days after giving birth. My father was afraid Anna's family would take the baby, so he wrapped him up and took him to his sister's house. Anna's family did take the baby away, but Albert died a few days later from the influenza.

Both Anna and the baby are buried in the old Monongahela Cemetery in Braddock, on the left side of the old chapel. They are buried on the Spernak plot, with the Krzyzosiak name on the markers on their graves.

My father worked at various jobs and learned many skills. During this time, he started to learn the construction trade and how to build houses. He was quite artistic and also learned how to do inlaid designs in hardwood floors. In 1919, he was hired for a job as an iron-worker to erect electrical cables on high towers in France. He was interested in the job and was anxious to go there. He got his passport on July 12, 1919. Unfortunately, as he was finalizing his travel plans to France, there was another family tragedy that left sadness deep within him.

My father's older sister, Victoria (Vic) lost her husband in a tragic accident in the Edgar Thompson Steel Mill. She had been married since 1902, had five children and was expecting her sixth child. A furnace at the mill exploded. Her husband and two other men were burnt to death, instantaneously. Four other men died from burns within a few days and four more men died from their injuries within the month. It was a terrible accident. The company paid a generous sum of seventy-five dollars toward the funeral expenses. Anthony was born after his father's death. I don't think Aunt Vic received any other type of compensation, but her sons were given jobs at the mill once they were old enough to work. Ironically, Anthony worked there all of his life and retired from the Edgar Thompson Steel Mill.

Just before planning to leave for France, my father met a beautiful young girl by the name of Helen Figulski, and his plans changed. They eloped and were married in Wellsburg, West Virginia, on September 20, 1920. Their first child, my older sister, Irene Marie Krzyzosiak, was born on June 25, 1921. My husband, Walter and Irene shared the very same birthday.

During the early years of their marriage, my father worked for Eichleay Brothers. He would take barges down the Ohio River from Pittsburgh, sometimes going all of the way down the Mississippi River to New Orleans. He loved that job as once again, my father was on the water like when he was a child floating on logs on the Monongahela, or when he was in the Navy. He always spoke of the time he spent on the barges and the stories of his adventures on the mighty Mississippi. He loved the job, but he found he was away from home for a few weeks at a time. With a young bride and trying to start a family, my father decided to take a job at the Westinghouse Electric factory in East Pittsburgh. When there were lay-offs during the depression or a labor union strike, my father would build houses. At that time, there was no written contract, just a friendly, honest handshake.

For only completing the third grade, my father did quite well and accomplished many things in his life. He built several beautiful homes and was able to completely rebuild just about any automobile. Nearly all of his skills were self-taught. My father had two complete sets of encyclopedias. One set was on building houses and the other set was on auto mechanics and repair. When he was dating my mother, he owned an Indian motorcycle. My father's first automobile was an Essex, which my mother referred to as an "ass-ache," as it wasn't too comfortable or too dependable. Auto repair was a hobby that he truly loved to do. He called these encyclopedias, his "Bibles" and probably knew every word as he read them many times from cover to cover.

Our home was the first house my father completely built. He finished it in 1922. Prior to living there, my parents and Irene lived on the third floor at the home of her mother and father. While building our house, he also installed indoor plumbing in the house of my uncle, Charles Figulski.

When my parents were first married, several of my Father's nephews would come and stay with them for a few weeks in the summer. Many of them lived in the city and more urban areas like Braddock. Turtle Creek at that time, and especially where my parents lived on the Electric Plan hill, was considered to be "out in the country." There were woods and many open fields. It was the perfect place for children to run and play. My father's oldest sister, Anne Szymoroski, had two boys, Charles and Len. They were frequent summer time guests. They enjoyed playing in the open spaces and had a great time. Both Charles and Len went on to become graduates of West Point and had lifetime military careers, both being Brigadier Generals. They had fond memories of those summer visits in the country with Uncle Joe. My father's brother, Max used to also send his son, Chuckie, to stay with my parents every summer. I remember his visits when I was growing up. My father always sent Chuckie home with a pair of new shoes for school. One day, just before my father passed away, Chuckie came to see him. He told him that he never forgot his summer visits to the country and that he was so thankful for my father's kindness to him. My father's nephew, Anthony was also a summer time visitor. My Father always felt a special kinship to Anthony, as he was born after his father was killed in the steel mill accident. My mother once recalled riding with Anthony on the open-air street car to Turtle Creek from Braddock. Everyone remarked about his beautiful head full of ringlet curls and they would ask her the age of the little girl.

Over many years, my father built thirteen more homes, plus numerous additions, garages, and other various carpenter projects. Another of his proud accomplishments was designing a conveyor system for the Millikin Brickyards in Pitcairn, Pennsylvania. My father not only designed the system, but he made most of the parts and installed it. Through the years, if the system would fail, sure enough, my father would get a phone call from them and before you would know it, he'd be out there tinkering with it. When I was very small, my father was asked to help lay concrete blocks for an ice house that was being built in Turtle Creek. Everyone knew of his building talents and would always ask for my father's help. He was always happy to oblige.

My father enjoyed keeping busy. The garage and basement workshops were his domain. Everyone knew exactly where they could find him - either working on a project in the basement or under a car in the garage. Nephews, cousins and neighborhood boys would gather and watch him work for hours. He loved talking with them and they loved talking to him. Whether my father was working on a car or doing a plumbing project, young Stanley Figulski liked to watch him and hand him the tools he needed. Stanley always said he learned so much from my father and the knowledge he gained stayed with him all his life. He, along with the other boys, spent many hours with my father and enjoyed him immensely.

During the 1930's, my father converted the engine on our Model A Ford to burn kerosene. It seemed to work to his satisfaction on short distance trips. We were planning a trip to visit Uncle John and Aunt Florence in Philadelphia. My father thought this would be the perfect time to test this latest invention. My mother's reply was "Absolutely NOT....No, No, No. The girls and I will not ride that far in that car. We could be blown to Hell and back!" Much to my father's disappointment, that settled that.

When my sister and I each married and started to have children, my father was in his glory. He loved his grandchildren very much and enjoyed making things with them. There are many fond memories of my father and the grandchildren at his workbench. Not just the boys, he included my daughter, Bonnie as well. My father called her, his little "Princess" and loved treating her like one. One winter, my father built a large detailed model of the Queen Mary ocean liner. He even wired lights into the staterooms. My mother proudly displayed it on the fireplace mantle for a long time.

During the war, certain things were very scarce, especially those made of metal. One simply could not buy a metal Radio wagon for the boys, as none could be found. This did not discourage my father. He built wagons made of wood for Irene's son, Jackie, and for my son, Ronnie. I don't know where he ever managed to find the wheels for them, but he did. Eventually, he even made them little racers. Whenever my father bought toys, he bought the exact same for each child. Whenever he bought something for the house, he bought the very same for both Irene and for me. My father was all about fairness.

Another time, my father made a whirly gig of a man sawing wood for the kids to enjoy watching. The harder the wind blew, the faster the man would saw. It was mounted on the corner of the roof of my parents' garage in plain sight from the back porch and the kitchen door. The kids watched the whirly gig for hours. He showed such great ingenuity in most of the things he made. I often wonder whatever became of these treasures. Most of them disappeared after my mother sold their home. One can only wonder if the people who took them ever really appreciated their meaning and value.

Every year, my father created an elaborate display underneath the Christmas tree. Working in the basement, he would start on the display months ahead of time. It consisted of a village with an electric train going through it. My father was so particular, that he hand-painted the little houses and figures and wired everything to light up. At one point, he fashioned a snow covered mountain complete with downhill skiers, on a motorized belt. Each year, the display changed and grew a little more elaborate than the year before. My father loved the holidays, especially Christmas. He mentioned when he was a child, he would look into the windows of the fine Victorian homes in Braddock. Those who lived there were much more fortunate than he was as a child. They had large Christmas trees that were richly decorated and the rooms were lavishly trimmed. There were beautiful gifts under the tree. My father vowed he would provide a better life for his children than what he experienced. He always said "A person is what he makes of himself by being honest and working very hard." My father never sympathized with anyone's excuse for failure, or that it was "because they didn't have parents." He strongly believed in and lived by "The Golden Rule…Do unto others as you would have them do unto you." During his lifetime, my father did many kind deeds to help someone in need. Several times, during the height of the depression, he arranged for a load of coal to be delivered to a nearby neighbor who had no money. I'm not sure if they ever knew it was sent by my father, but he knew then, that they had warmth on a cold winter's night.

My father liked the Tarzan movies. When one was playing at the Capitol Theatre in Braddock, he would take the boys and his little "Princess," too. Kenny, my second son, was so much younger, but he still has fond memories of the times spent with his grandpap. He took the kids to the Ice Capades when the show came to town, as well as the rodeo. There wasn't a summer that went by that didn't find my father and the kids at the zoo, the county fair, and of course, Kennywood amusement park. We always had picnics and celebrated the Fourth of July with sparklers and other fireworks.

In later years, when Irene, Jack and their two boys moved in with my parents, the house at 612 Locust Street was once again, a very busy place. Along with them, came their dog, Smokey, a medium sized black spaniel mix. My father and Smokey were inseparable. Smokey loved him more than anyone else. Every day, when Smokey saw the neighborhood kids walking by on their way home from school at three o'clock, he knew my father would be coming home from work very shortly. Smokey would walk down Locust Street and sit and wait on the corner by the elementary school, watching for my father's Ford. My father would stop and open the car door for Smokey to get in for the ride home. Smokey's tail would not stop wagging until he walked into the kitchen with my father. Smokey thought that was the greatest thing. When the kids were old enough to go with my father for an ice cream treat to Dairy Delight in Turtle Creek, Smokey would go along and enjoy his very own ice cream cone. I guess Smokey was making up for the childhood dog that my father never had. My father and Smokey were such great pals.

My father did not believe in the sport of hunting and he was very adamant about it. He did not believe anyone had the right to take the life of an innocent animal. My father felt animals were a part of nature and should be left alone to be enjoyed. There was always enough food from the garden and the grocery markets. This caused difficulty with Irene's boys as they liked to go hunting. My father was not happy with this and the boys would sneak out of house through one of the basement windows with their hunting equipment. My father would have been very upset if he knew what they were up to.

My father retired from the Westinghouse Electric Corporation on June 1, 1960 after thirty eight years of loyal service. He worked in the micarta works in Trafford and then in the circuit breaker division in the East Pittsburgh plant. Even though my father was a very dedicated employee, he would have been more content working in a shipyard, building houses or working at a job outdoors or on the water. My mother would not move away from her family in Turtle Creek. I believe my father would have been happier if they had moved away and made other decisions earlier in their lives.

On the day my father retired, a photo was taken with his co-workers and supervisors. A luncheon was going to be held in his honor. My mother looked out of the back door to see him coming up the walk from the garage. She said, "My goodness, Joe, the luncheon is over awfully early. What happened?" My father said, "Those sons of bitches didn't eat with me for thirty eight years, so why would they think I want to eat with them today? They can shove their lunch up their asses!"

He was definitely his own kind of person and did things his own way. When my father wasn't working, he would be found wearing white dress shirts and often ties. He loved ties and hats and tended to be stylish in his dress. In the evenings, he would wear a satin smoking jacket with a velvet collar. My father loved reading, enjoyed listening to music and watching television in its early days. He enjoyed an occasional alcoholic beverage or beer, and smoking unfiltered Camel cigarettes. When he would like to sneak off, he would tell my mother that he had to take the car and "put fresh air in the tires." He loved to go to the V.F.W. and local dance clubs, to watch people doing the twist, the cha-cha, or the limbo, which was becoming popular then.

One evening, in May of 1961, my father was sitting with all of us on the back porch, enjoying a pleasant evening. For May, it was unseasonably warm. He had spent most of the afternoon working on his 1958 Ford, in the garage. As he put a cigarette into the corner of his mouth, about to light it, it dropped and rolled to the floor. My father suffered a devastating stroke and his life was never the same. He passed away nearly nine years later on January 13, 1970.

How sad it was that we could not enjoy him in a better way in the last years of his life. How sad it is he is not with us now to enjoy my grandchildren and to sit and have a smoke on the back porch.

My father, relaxing after a hard day's work, in 1955.

My Mother, Helen Figulski and Her Family

My mother, Helen Figulski, was born on January 19, 1901, in the village of Tarrs, a small mining town outside of Mt. Pleasant, Pennsylvania. Both of her parents were Polish immigrants. Her mother's maiden name was Marcianna Lewandowski, and she was from the village of Inowroclaw, in Poland. Her father's name was Joseph Figulski, and he was from Warsaw.

Marcianna came to America, alone at the age of eight, in 1886. There were some people aboard ship who were from the same village in Poland, so they kept an eye on her. Her mother had died and her father remarried and her step brothers and step sisters were very mean to her. They would tell her that their mother would poison her. She was the youngest child from the first marriage, and it was decided that she would be sent to America to live with an aunt in Mt. Pleasant. She would tell us of how frightened she was, to be going so far away from her father, brothers, and sisters. But she would not miss the threats and bad treatment from the new family. They put a sign around her neck which had instructions and her destination. Marcianna had only a few belongings in a cloth sack. She was scared to death. At this point in her life, she spoke no English. She was in the steerage section in the bottom of the ship, and was sick nearly the entire time because of rough seas. However, others on board, especially the older people and those from her village were kind and looked after her during the journey. Marcianna always said that if it wasn't for them, she may have not survived the trip. She never saw any of her family or visited her homeland again. In later years, she corresponded with one of her sisters who still lived in Poland. A family friend visited Poland years later and did bring a vial of soil for her grave.

In Mt. Pleasant, her aunt kept boarders in her home and Marcianna, my grandmother, ended up being no more than a servant. Not only did she work very hard for her aunt, but she was kept in rags. She was abused and neglected. After living there for a couple of years, she would sneak to church without her aunt knowing. One cold and snowy Christmas Eve, she went to church. My grandmother had no shoes and she wore a very thin, worn shawl to keep her warm. The priest waited outside of the church for her to leave, so he could question her about where she was living. He then took her back to the aunt's home and told her aunt that she would no longer be living there. The priest took her to his housekeeper's home, where she would live for the next couple of years. They were very kind and good to my grandmother. At last, she had a place to stay where she was no longer abused. She did chores for the housekeeper, for the priest, and in the church. Some of our family members attend that same church in Mt. Pleasant to this day.

My grandmother was nearly fifteen years old, when one day the priest from the church approached her. There was a nice, hardworking man who was looking to take a wife. This man was Joseph Figulski, who was born in 1867. He was twenty eight years old. They were married on Valentine's Day. She was so small, that when they went to get their marriage license in Greensburg, she had to stand on a box to answer the court clerk's questions. Over the years, they had ten children, and lost two babies. One baby named Martin, died during childbirth. He is buried in the Polish cemetery in Mt Pleasant. Tadeaus was an infant when he died, but his remains were later moved to Saint Joseph's Cemetery in North Versailles. Life in those days was quite different than it is today. There was much toil and hardship.

Joseph and his young wife settled into a company house, in Tarrs, Pennsylvania, outside of Mt. Pleasant. Joseph worked very hard in the coal mines, where eventually, two of their older sons joined him. It was a very difficult and dangerous occupation. They would come home exhausted from a day's work and literally black from the coal dust. Joseph and Marcianna did not want to see this same kind of life for their children. It was nothing more than a vicious trap. The company that owned the mines, owned the homes, and owned the company store where the miners and their families purchased food and supplies. By the time the mining company deducted the rent and the bill from the company store from the paycheck, there was very little left. It was extremely difficult to save any money to get out of that trap.

Joseph and Marcianna started their family in 1895 with the birth of their oldest child, Charles. Next, Joseph was born in 1897, then Clinton, in 1899. My mother, Helen, the first girl, was born in 1901. Next, there was Regina (Jean), born in 1902, Irene in 1908, Dorothy in 1911, Edna in 1913, Elizabeth (Betty) in 1915 and then, Warren who was born in 1918. Betty who is 94 years old, is the only one living at the time of this writing. It was a large family, full of lots of love.

My mother, Helen had great memories of growing up in Tarrs. It was quite rural and isolated, surrounded by woods, meadows, streams, and creeks. It was a perfectly beautiful place to spend a childhood. At that time, most of Pennsylvania was still very rural, except for the larger cities and railroad towns. When Helen and the children weren't helping their mother with the other babies or housework, they would play in the open fields and woods. They would pick berries and summer wildflowers. My mother and her sister, Jean were close playmates and had many adventures together. She often told us of a woman named Mrs. Rainey, who was a bit eccentric and constantly carried an umbrella. Mrs. Rainey used to yell and chase Helen and Jean and swing her umbrella at them. They were afraid of her. One day when she was chasing them, they ran along the top of an ash pile. Mrs. Rainey lost her footing and slid down the pile, all the way to the bottom. My mother and Jean didn't look back, but continued to run all the way home.

My mother attended a one-room schoolhouse with the rest of her brothers and sisters. The teacher was very nice and she knew that the parents were poor miners or local farmers. One day, while my mother and Jean were walking home from school, a terrible storm came up suddenly. Thunder was booming and lightening was striking off in the distance. The little girls were afraid and started to hurry home. My mother had an umbrella, so if the rain started, they could stay partially dry. All of a sudden, it began to rain, so they opened the umbrella. They were crossing a creek on a foot bridge, when all of a sudden, there was a bright flash followed immediately by a very loud boom. The next thing Jean knew was that my mother was lying on the bridge. The umbrella was completely gone. After a second or two, my mother stood up and got her bearings. The water under the bridge acted as the perfect conductor for the lightening. When it struck my mother, it knocked her to the ground and pulled the umbrella straight up out of her hands in a ball of flames. Her arm was numb for a few days, but she never forgot it. From then on, every time a storm was coming with thunder rumbling and lightening crackling in the distant sky, my mother would calmly say, "Let's go inside the house." We all knew why.

My mother remembered a lot about Christmas. They would have special meals and fruits and nuts as treats. She would also mention "All Hallow's Eve," before the days of Halloween and trick or treat, when children were put directly to bed after dinner and the shades were pulled tight. There were a lot of superstitions.

My mother, Helen Figulski, in 1908.

Upon the birth of Dorothy in 1911, my grandparents planned a small christening celebration. She was christened at the church in Mt. Pleasant, and a special meal was to follow at their home. There were traveling gypsies in the area that got wind of the celebration. They decided to join in the festivities. The gypsies burst into my grandparents' home, playing violins and dancing, to celebrate the birth of Dorothy. They caused such a commotion, but claimed they were there with good tidings of joy for the baby and my grandparents. As the gypsies danced through the house, each time they passed the dining room table, more of the breaded pork chops on the large platter, disappeared. The gypsies left as quickly as they came. Everyone there sat back in amazement. The breaded pork chops that my grandmother prepared that morning were completely gone. When my grandmother was no longer using her china dishes, everyone in the family was given a piece or two, as a remembrance. I was the fortunate one to receive the very same meat platter that the pork chops were stacked on that day. Along with it, goes the story of the gypsies. I also have her gravy boat and still proudly display both pieces in our china cabinet.

The hardworking immigrants were nothing but a gift to the millionaire industrialists who used the immigrants to build their personal wealth and huge corporations. A prominent Pittsburgh family owned the mines, and everything that went along with them, including my grandparents. All of the vast wealth of these industrialists came directly from the hardships, sweat, and deaths of many, many poor men and boys. In the 1930's, my grandfather died from the miner's or black lung disease which he contracted from the many years he spent toiling in the coal mines. At the time, there was no type of compensation for black lung disease. Lawsuits or settlements didn't exist. In the 1990s, the opulent mansion of one of the industrialists in Pittsburgh, was restored to its heyday and former glory. Tours of the mansion and the beautiful surrounding gardens were available to the public. The gardens were available for weddings and special events. Out of respect for my ancestry, I would never set foot on that property, as it is nothing more than a slap in the face to what that family did to the immigrants. The mansion was built on the lives of many poor immigrants and their hardships and strife should never be forgotten.

There were many accidents in the mines in those days. There were no laws about unsafe conditions or child labor. It was a very dangerous place to work. The men took caged canary birds into the mines to alert them of gas leaks. The Pennsylvania countryside was not only full of coal fields, but also abundant with natural gas. My mother remembered her father's miner's cap with the primitive carbide light, and his metal lunch pail.

One time, there was an explosion and cave-in at the mine, and all the men scrambled to get out. My grandfather was working in the mine that day and so was his oldest son, Charles. Amidst all of the mayhem at the entrance of the mine, Charles was trying frantically to locate his father. All of a sudden, Charles turned around to see him standing behind him. My grandfather was trying to find his son. He was afraid Charles was still inside of the mine. They both escaped tragedy that day.

There was another explosion and cave-in at the mine. In this one, my grandfather wasn't so fortunate. Charles was not able to find his father as he was still inside of the mine. My grandfather was extricated from the rubble, but had lost an eye in the blast. He was hospitalized at Westmoreland Hospital in Greensburg. My grandmother walked to Mt. Pleasant, from their village to get a trolley into Greensburg to visit him. After he recovered, he was allowed to return to his shift at the mine. Little did he know his employment at the mine was nearly over, and that their lives were about to change forever.

One day a traveling salesman, selling religious articles and pictures came through Tarrs with his wares. My grandmother lamented to him about my grandfather's accident and the fact that they were unhappy with their situation. He told them of a wonderful, life changing solution. The salesman spoke of a little town east of Pittsburgh, where a man recently opened an electrical factory. The work was plentiful and under safe conditions, with good pay. He spoke of the many opportunities there, and of the thriving small towns growing in the valley, near the electrical plant. The owner of the electrical plant was George Westinghouse, and his plant began manufacturing the electric motors for trolley cars, among other things.

My grandfather and the older sons took a trip to this town by train, to investigate what the salesman had told them. They found it all to be true. Plans were made and the days of toiling at the mine would soon be over. It was decided that Charles would be the first to leave the mine and move away to work in the Westinghouse Electric plant. He filed an application for employment and was hired immediately. He moved away and started working there. Charles was so happy to be away from the mine. Shortly thereafter, in early 1913, the rest of the family moved, leaving the terrible trap of the mine behind.

My mother told us of how the family was moved. All of their furniture and belongings were loaded on a very large horse-drawn wagon and sent ahead. My grandparents and all of the children rode the train, and arrived at East Pittsburgh station. For a short time, they rented a house high on a hill in Chalfant Borough, overlooking the town of East Pittsburgh and the Westinghouse plant. The children would walk about a mile and a half to attend Gilmore School. My mother remembered how far it was to walk to school and how steep the hills were, especially in the winter.

When my grandfather applied for employment at the Westinghouse plant, it was required that one must be fluent in the English language. One had to be able to read, write and speak English and be able to communicate with your co-workers and supervisors. After all, this was America, and assimilation into society and its work force could only be expected of all immigrants. That even applied when you went to the store to buy groceries and supplies. None of the displays or labels were furnished in other languages. It was long before this time, that both of my grandparents spoke, read and wrote proper English. They assimilated very well into their new society and were very proud to be Americans.

Eventually, throughout the years, everyone in the family including me worked at the Westinghouse plant. My mother's youngest brother, Warren was the only one who didn't work there. He did quite well for himself. Warren started working in the meat department at Kroger's grocery store when he was just out of high school. Before his retirement from Kroger's, he was the president of the meat buyers for the organization. Charles stayed with Westinghouse and retired after nearly fifty years of service. He was very involved in the community and served on the school board for 28 years, retiring as the president. Joseph started working at the plant and was quickly promoted, eventually going into a management position for Westinghouse in Buffalo, New York. Clinton followed in the same footsteps as Joseph, starting at Westinghouse and eventually ending up in management in Lester, outside of Philadelphia. My mother and her sister, Jean worked on the production floor, winding coils on the electric motors. They worked there until they married. Irene worked in wiring and taping. She found herself as a supervisor in Atlanta, Georgia, during World War II at a factory that had been converted to bomber production. Dorothy worked in an office position and Edna worked in production at the East Pittsburgh. The youngest sister, Betty worked in the printing department.

In 1916, when my mother was fifteen years old, she started working at the Westinghouse Electric plant. She was so proud of the fact that when she and her sister, Jean were winding coils on the production floor, she made fourteen cents an hour. At the same time, my grandfather made eleven cents an hour. In those days, there were strict rules to follow including a dress code, even on the production floor. There were no labor laws but Mr. Westinghouse took good care of his employees. He expected a hard day's work in return. Some of the work was called piece work as you got paid according to how many pieces you did.

Everyone in the entire family was very ambitious and had strong, dedicated work ethics. There was a small lane on one side of the Westinghouse plant in East Pittsburgh that was actually named Figulski Way because everyone in the family worked there. My grandmother was so proud of her family and how hard they worked.

After working at the Westinghouse plant for a while, my grandfather and Charles saved enough money to buy property and build houses that they would actually own. Just to the east of the Westinghouse plant, another small town called Turtle Creek was beginning to grow.

The borough of Turtle Creek, was incorporated into a town in 1892, and had a very historic past. The original inhabitants of the valley were a small tribe of the Delaware Indians. The small valley was secluded and lush with woodlands. There were natural caves that the Indians used as shelter. Hunting and fishing was plentiful, and the large creek that wound its way through the small valley was full of snapping turtles. The Indians would catch the turtles and eat the meat, or use the meat in stew or soup. The Indians referred to the large creek as "Turtle River," and tried to keep others from settling there. Traveling west was very difficult in those days and many of the early settlers perished due to disease or Indian attacks. Many paths through the surrounding woods were created by the Delaware Indians as hunting trails and amazingly, centuries later, they still exist today. We referred to the paths as the Indian Paths. We would often play there as children, as did my children.

The first white man to inhabit the valley was a fur trader named John Frazer. He did blacksmith work and developed a good relationship with the Indians. He understood and spoke many of their languages. He was useful to the Indians as a blacksmith for their horses, and also with his knowledge as a gunsmith.

Eventually, the little valley was not as quiet as it once was. Soldiers during the time of the French and Indian War, and later, the Revolutionary War, passed through the valley, on their way between forts and battles. Soon the small Delaware tribe disappeared.

A large fort was soon established in Pittsburgh, and was a major stop on the way westward. There wasn't much beyond the fort, and it remained that way for many years. The route to Fort Pitt from Philadelphia was soon established, and it became accessible by stage coach. In those days, it would take twenty days to make the journey, provided the weather was good and there were no mishaps along the way. Turtle Creek became the first stagecoach stop east of Pittsburgh, on the way east to Philadelphia, or the last stagecoach stop heading west to Pittsburgh, Fort Pitt, and Fort Duquesne.

The first land grant in Turtle Creek was given to a woman named Martha Myers, in 1769. The parcel of land was referred to as "the Widow's Dower", and it was there, that she owned and operated the Wayside Inn. It was basically a tavern serving food and drink, offering sleeping accommodations, and a livery to rest and water horses. In the years to follow, the road west greatly improved and so did the traffic. Widow Myers supported herself and four children, nicely, by operating the inn. In fact, it is written in George Washington's journals, dated 1770 that he dined with the widow, Martha Myers, at the Wayside Inn along the Turtle Creek.

In 1817, Henry Chalfant, bought the Wayside Inn from the widow Myers. A post office was established there in 1832. It is from that point on, the town started to materialize around the Wayside Inn. There was a blacksmith shop, then a general store. In a short time, there was a bakery, a cobbler, and a barber shop. Social life revolved around the inn. The people of the town and travelers would gather there. They would enjoy sharing conversation and discuss traveling conditions along the stage route, current events, and politics. When it would rain or snow or the creek would flood, the unpaved roads would turn into a muddy bog. Eventually, wooden sidewalks were built, as well as a plank road.

In 1850, big changes came to the little valley. The railroad was coming through on its way to Pittsburgh, from Philadelphia. This would mark the beginning of the industrial revolution. This also was a major deciding factor when George Westinghouse selected the location of the new electric plant. The 500 acres along the Pennsylvania railroad line was ideal. The nearby creek provided water and drainage. The proximity to the coal mines was important for fuel. In 1894, Westinghouse opened his first production shop there in a single brick building.

Turtle Creek was the up and coming town. This is was where my grandparents and Charles decided they wanted to settle. They went to the land office and purchased two pieces of property side by side, high on a hill that was once part of Patton Township. It was approximately a mile and a half through the woods from the Westinghouse Electric plant in East Pittsburgh. Its rural setting reminded them of the peaceful country life they so enjoyed outside of Mt. Pleasant. It was just beautiful. From certain areas, one commanded a picturesque view of the Turtle Creek Valley below.

Charles was the first to build a home on the property, as he had just married Mary Panzchek, who was from the nearby town of Braddock. My grandparents completed their home about one year later, in 1915. Elizabeth was born there, just after they moved in. She was so small, that my Grandmother carried her on a pillow. Their home was a large three story, brick, house with big front and back porches, and a concrete basement. There was still no electricity on the hill that was now known as the Electric Plan. The lighting was gas and the heating was coal or a wood fire in the winter.

One day, a man came around from the Maytag washing machine company in Newton, Iowa. He told them that if they purchased a washing machine, the company would act as a sponsor for them, and it would expedite the hook up of electric power to their home. They all purchased washing machines, but it took two more years for the power to be hooked up. My grandmother would be in the basement boiling the laundry, getting it ready for her wash board and the fancy new electric Maytag washing machine sat a few feet away in a crate. It was a happy day for my grandmother, when she could at last use the washing machine. The entire family remained loyal to the Maytag brand.

When my mother was about twelve years old, she got a job as a cook's helper, at Rentler's Hotel in East Pittsburgh. She started working there in the evenings after school, and on weekends. The hotel and dining room were very busy. The Rentler's were German and most of the food they prepared was of German origin. My mother told us that this is where she had to learn how to make hasenpfeffer or rabbit stew. First, she had to learn how to skin and prepare the meat from freshly killed rabbits. She was not thrilled about that, but she learned. This is where she first developed her love for cooking and baking. Coincidently, Mrs. Rentler's nephew, Albert Rapp, married Dorothy, my mother's younger sister, years later.

My mother's formal education ended when she graduated from the eighth grade. At the time, children were fortunate if they even completed schooling at that level. It was then, that she decided to work at the Westinghouse plant, as that would be more beneficial to her and her family. Her younger sister, Jean, followed in her footsteps, winding coils on the production floor, after she finished the eighth grade. Younger sister, Irene did the same and joined the others at the Westinghouse plant. Two of my mother's older brothers, Joseph and Clinton, attended college, but they did not complete the course of study to get degrees. At the start of World War I, Joseph quit college to enlist in the Army. He spent most of that time in France, and returned home safely, at the end of the war. Joseph sent beautiful silk, embroidered aprons for all of the girls. My mother cherished the gift from him, and left it unused in the box. Upon her death, we discovered it. The apron had simply rotted away.

Dorothy, Edna, and Betty began working at the Westinghouse plant just as their siblings had before them. Unless women were planning on becoming nurses or teachers, higher education was not sought. Girls were meant to marry and have families.

The top of the Electric Plan hill was starting to become more sparsely populated. There was a two-story brick building that was a school known as the Electric Plan Elementary School, It was annexed from Patton Township in 1916. The school was there when Charles and my grandparents started building their homes. Many others had the same idea and more families left the farms and mines to come to the valley and work at the Westinghouse plant.

It was a very long walk from the top of the Electric Plan hill, down into the valley, to the Westinghouse plant. There were just Indian paths through the woods that went so far, then a small ash road that went into Turtle Creek. The walk could be quite an adventure, especially in bad weather. My mother, her brothers and sisters would leave the house very early every morning to make the trek into the valley below to go to work. A family named Chase bought the property behind my grandparents' home. They built a home and had a boarder, named Mauro Tummolo. He also worked at Westinghouse.

The homes of Uncle Charlie and my grandparents before
Cedar Avenue was paved, 1916.

When the snow started to fall and accumulate into its depths, Mauro and the other boys would walk ahead of the girls, stomping down the snow to make a path, so their long skirts would not get wet. It wasn't long after that when some of the boys constructed a large bobsled. They would all pile onto it and ride the entire way down into Turtle Creek at the bottom of Electric Plan hill. They had great fun riding to work in the morning on the bobsled, but remember, after work they had to pull it back up the hill.

With such a large family and a nice new home to take care of, there was always a lot of work to do. There were not many of the modern conveniences. Bread was baked fresh every morning. Chickens were kept for laying fresh eggs. My grandfather had been a gardener in Warsaw in his youth and definitely had a green thumb. Several fruit trees were planted and vegetables were grown. A lot of canning was done. My grandmother made delicious soups from the home-grown vegetables. My grandfather planted beautiful beds of roses for my grandmother. The roses are actually still blooming there today. He also had a large grape arbor and made wine from the grapes for holidays and other special occasions. The wine was stored in small wooden barrels in the basement. One time when they were entertaining company, they sent my mother to the basement with an empty glass bottle that she was to fill with wine for the guests. To fill the bottle, she had to use a siphon hose, using suction from her mouth. She had difficulty getting it to work and each time she would suck on the hose, she would get a mouthful of the tasty wine. By the time the bottle was filled and she took it back upstairs, she sat down by the stove in the kitchen and fell fast asleep. She probably had more wine in her than she put in the bottle.

The Figulski family was known to be a very quiet living family. They were humble and were appreciative of what life offered them. They worked very hard and were taught to enjoy a hard day's work, as you always reaped the benefits. They were proud Americans who rarely spoke in their native Polish language. Most of the children only spoke and understood English. They preserved the Polish customs of the special holidays and practiced the custom of extending great hospitality to any guest that entered their home. They truly entertained, using the best of manners and etiquette. The boys and girls were taught to have good manners and social graces and to never shame their families or themselves. They were taught habits of impeccable grooming and cleanliness. They were taught the importance of their appearance and always presented themselves properly. One would never know the children came from poor immigrant parents. They established a beautiful home on the hill, known as the Electric Plan.

Once, my mother's sister, Irene, came home with her beautiful long hair cut into a very stylish bob that was becoming popular in the early twenties. My grandfather went through the roof. He was so angry and told her that she looked like a boy. He was a loving father, but was very strict, especially when it came to the girls.

My grandmother really loved to dress up wearing beads and earrings, and she especially loved hats. She went to Lottie Aments Hat Shop in Turtle Creek, and always admired the latest fashion in hats. The winter snow would be falling and she would already have her new hat selected as soon as the spring arrivals came in. My grandmother liked fine things and had exquisite taste not only in clothing, but in her home as well.

She would send the girls into Turtle Creek to O'Neil's Dry Goods Store to buy fabrics and material to do sewing projects. With my grandmother's help, they would design patterns and try to mimic the latest fashions so the skirts, blouses, and dresses they had sewn looked like they came from a fine shop or a fancy department store.

I remember going up to the third floor with my grandmother when I was very small. She had a wind-up Victrola there, that she refused to part with. In the cabinet below the player, there were stacks of records that she had that were mostly symphony and opera. Her favorite was the great Caruso. I would wind up the Victrola and the records would play. We would be up there for hours, listening to the beautiful music. My grandmother was quite a lady. She was smart enough to know, that she would never be asked to join the local women's club but this was not important as she was very much more a lady in her own right.

After twelve years of working for the Westinghouse Electric plant, my grandfather could no longer work. His ability to breathe was diminishing rapidly. The years he spent working in the mine had caught up with him. Within the next couple of years, my grandfather deteriorated terribly. He became housebound as he could no longer walk up the hill from Turtle Creek. He could no longer tend to his vegetable and flower gardens. Then, it became a chore to climb the stairs to go to his bedroom at night. He was withering away from miner's lung disease, as they called it then, before it was known as black lung. A bed was set up for him in the corner of the dining room. You could hear him wheezing all through the house, as he struggled for every breath. He passed away in 1932. After my grandfather died, my grandmother and the family observed the proper period of mourning.

After a year or so, my grandmother had her hair cut short and got a permanent wave. She enjoyed going to the movies with anyone that would go with her. Sometimes, she went to the Olympic Theatre in Turtle Creek, or the Rivoli Theatre in East Pittsburgh. My grandmother loved musicals. Her all-time favorite movie was the epic "Gone with the Wind." No one knows for certain how many times she saw it. I know that I accompanied her at least on one occasion. After the show, on the way home, she always stopped at Jim's Soda Shop in Turtle Creek and got a banana split. To my grandmother, that was a wonderful evening out.

She loved to play bingo at Saint Colman's church. My grandmother also learned to play the illegal numbers game. She used to follow her Dream Book and place bets with bookies. Sometimes, she would send the boys to play her numbers with a bookie in Turtle Creek or East Pittsburgh. In fact, my husband was always happy to help her out with that.

My mother's co-worker and friend at the Westinghouse plant, Helen Najelca, lived in Braddock. One night after work, she invited my mother to go home with her for dinner. There was a trolley car that went to Braddock, so they would not have to walk there, but at a certain time, the trolley stopped running for the night. Helen assured her that someone with an automobile would drive her home after their supper. When the girls were walking up the sidewalk to the porch of Helen's house, there was a handsome young man, Joseph Krzyzosiak, sitting on the railing of the porch of the house next door. Helen introduced them and he drove my mother back to end of the ash road on Electric Plan, after dinner. I guess that was officially their first date. They began dating. Several months later, they eloped to Wellsburg, West Virginia. They were married on September 9, 1920. Her parents were not very happy, as they wanted her to have a proper church wedding with a party reception at their home. My mother's younger sister, Jean, just married Andrew Shogan in August.

My mother, Helen Figulski, in 1917.

They had given her a proper church wedding and a beautiful party afterwards. Their finances after that could not provide my mother with the same, only a month later. To appease my grandparents, they were later married in a simple ceremony at Saint Colman's church in Turtle Creek.

My parents moved into the two rooms on the third floor of my grandparents' home on the hill, known as the Electric Plan, in Turtle Creek.

The official address was 1611 Cedar Avenue. They were the first of many newlywed couples in the family that started housekeeping in those two rooms. Nearly everyone in the family started there, including me.

My father saved some money and was able to purchase a small piece of property, only a few hundred yards from my grandparents' home. He was working on the barges at the time, and making good money. My mother was expecting their first baby. On June 25, 1921, Irene was born.

Once Irene was born, my father quit the job delivering barges. He was hired at the Westinghouse plant. My parents started building their own home. My mother worked right along side of my father, so the house could be finished sooner. At one point, she actually suffered a fall from scaffolding when she was helping him one day. My mother blamed the development of premature diabetes on the result of internal injuries she had from the fall. Nevertheless, after a few days to recover, she was back on the job by the side of her husband, to finish the construction of their home. This was really the start of my father's career as a home builder. Within a couple of years, my mother's brother, Joseph and his wife, Anne, then my mother's sister, Jean and her husband, Andy, approached my father about building houses for them. They both also purchased lots, again only a few hundred yards from my grandparents' home. That was the best part about growing up there. We were surrounded by family. There were aunts, uncles, and grandparents, not to mention, many cousins. There were family get-togethers constantly. How fortunate could one person be!

Irene was still a small baby, when my parents moved into their newly built home, at 612 Locust Street in 1922. My father was still completing construction on the garage which was situated behind the house. Eventually, there was to be an ash alley there that would run down to the concrete wall of the Electric Plan Elementary School.

My mother told my sister and me about making moonshine liquor, as many of the other people living there were also making it. It was meant to be a fun project for them and not meant to make money. After all, this was starting to be the very beginning of the prohibition era. One day, there was a knock at the front door, and my mother answered it. Much to her shock, there stood a federal government revenue agent. He told my mother he stopped there just simply on a routine visit, but he smelled yeast. The agent wanted to know exactly what she was doing. Luckily, she had just baked fresh bread that morning, and had two loaves cooling on the kitchen table. She replied to him that she was baking bread. Then little Irene started crying. My mother told the agent she had no time to continue to talk with him, as the baby was crying and needed her. She promptly closed the door. That night, my father and mother disassembled the small still that they had been operating in their basement. They carried the mash in a wash tub, up to a sewer and dumped it all in. My father was about to pour some of the concrete floor in the garage. They took the pieces of the still and buried them deep into a pit that my father was putting in the floor of the garage. They poured the concrete the very next day over the top of the still. I guess their secret is probably still buried there. All of us would laugh about it many times through the years. They took many chances in their lives, but had a lot of fun and many laughs in doing so.

At the very top of the Electric Plan hill, there were once a lot of mine pits. At the very end of Locust Street, there was an entrance to one of the closed mines, which was once owned by the McKinney family. Another entrance to another mine was on the side of a steep hill, way above the lower Monroeville Road. There were abundant droppings of coal to be found around the entrances to the mines. My mother and father, and Anne and Clare Campbell, their close friends, used to walk together with pails to pick up coal. They would take the coal home, and burn it in the little heatrola heaters. The heaters would supplement the warmth provided by the main coal furnace in the house.

I was born on December 2, 1925. On my birth certificate, I was officially named as Marcyanna, after my grandmother. Since my sister was named after my mother's sister, Irene, my father wanted me to be named after someone in his family. My name was then changed to Maryann Barbara. Barbara was his mother's first name. The Figulski family always remained tightly bonded, even though many of us are now separated by years and miles. My grandparents had such a strong respect for their heritage and family. It was always of utmost importance to honor and keep the customs and traditions of the family alive. One of the most important traditions was to use the customary family christening dress that my grandmother purchased many years ago when she had her first baby, Charles, in 1895. It consisted of a lovely long white shirt with lace and a ribbon of embroidery, and all of her children were baptized in it. It was passed down in the family for all of the babies to be baptized in. It is now over one hundred years old, starting to shred, and can no longer be laundered. The last person, who had possession of the dress, was Regina Mandela of Scottsdale, Arizona. She was the daughter of Charles, the first baby to use the gown.

Elizabeth (Betty) was the youngest daughter to marry in 1937. She and her husband, Joe, took residence in grandmother's house and continue to live there at the time of this writing. My grandmother spent her remaining years, living happily with them, and helping Betty with her young family. We all have such wonderful memories of my grandmother. I always remember her humor and the kindness of her heart. Often times, she would visit with all of us in our homes, and offer her assistance in caring for our young children. In 1954, after watching her favorite show on television, The Liberace Show, she told Betty to send in a request for one of her favorite songs, to be played on the show. After that, she went upstairs to get ready to go to bed for the evening. Suddenly, she collapsed and died. She had a good marriage and provided endless love to her family and survived a childhood with great courage. She made a life for herself and her family that was much better than she ever thought it would be. She will never be forgotten. The Figulski family plot is at St. Joseph's Cemetery in East McKeesport. My mother and her brothers and sisters tried to continue with the traditions and the family closeness that was created by their parents. Holidays and special celebrations still continued to be shared with close family members.

My mother was a lot of fun. She loved to entertain and certainly continued with the family tradition of hospitality. My parents' kitchen was the place to be for social activity. There was always hot coffee and sweets to eat. One would not be in the backdoor for a second or two, before my mother would say, "Let me get something for you or…. Can I make you a sandwich?" She loved to play cards, mostly pinochle and rummy. Her lady-friends loved to come to play cards, as they knew that she would serve something delicious. The kitchen was her domain, and she would put Julia Child to shame. She loved cooking and baking and made something every day. She helped to preserve the customs of Polish cuisine that her mother taught her. She taught both Irene and I to do the same. Like her mother, she enjoyed the movies and loved reading the movie magazines and following the Hollywood Stars of the day.

After I was born, she began to develop a problem with obesity that would follow her through her entire life. Her weight was like a roller coaster, as it would go up and down, until the time of her death. Even though she died from congestive heart failure, the cause of her death on her death certificate was listed as obesity. She did battle with diabetes and its effects, from a young age. In later years, even after cataract surgery, she had bad vision due to the diabetes. She was not only a food lover, but also a food addict. When she died, she was only about a size twelve. When my father met and married her, she was a striking, thin, beautiful girl. She had exquisite features, with dark hair and dark eyes. It was sad to see how her diet and her illness affected her health. Her heart and soul were what really mattered the most. She was a wonderful mother, a teacher to her children and grandchildren, and a good friend and neighbor. She had many friends, that she had known all of her life. She enjoyed a good conversation and could talk for hours. Even though she had a limited formal education, she was quite intelligent and could keep up with the best of them. She was generally a sweet lady, but could command the use of a very sharp tongue when she needed to. She was a woman of convictions and opinions.

Even though, she had a weight problem, she was very fastidious about her appearance. She wouldn't leave the bedroom, unless her hair was properly fixed, she was wearing earrings, and had on face powder. My mother only wore dresses around the house when she was working. She was just as fussy about our home. She developed her housekeeping skills and decorating taste from her mother. She loved the finer things such as good table linens, silver and hand-painted china dishes, fine furniture and nice window treatments. My mother would always say that people could tell what a house was like on the inside by the way the windows looked on the outside. Sadly, my mother passed away on March 24, 1977. My parents were both laid to rest in the Penn Lincoln Cemetery in North Huntingdon Township, Pennsylvania.

Growing Up
and the Great Depression

My sister, Irene and I were so lucky to have the kind of childhood that we did. We were blessed with good and loving parents and many wonderful relatives who lived close by. We could sit on the back porch of our house and see our grandparent's house, then to the left was Uncle Charlie's house, and to the left of his house, was Uncle Joe's house. To the right of my grandparents' house, and a little further beyond, was Aunt Jean's house. It was one huge extended family and we had so many happy times together.

In the 1920s, the pavement on Locust Street ended just beyond our house, past the intersection of Cedar Avenue where my grandparents' house was located. Locust Street turned into a narrow, ash road that went on for another block, then, at the intersection of Beech Street, it turned into a dirt road which became a path into the woods. There was a large pond with frogs, tadpoles and salamanders. The Indian path to the right side of the pond went further up the hill to a plateau, where there were beautiful open fields and meadows surrounded by more woods. It was such a beautiful and perfect place for children to play.

When we were young, we didn't venture far from our house or from the homes of our relatives. All of the girls would get together and play house with our dolls. We would dress up in our mothers' old clothes and fancy high heeled shoes. We had such great fun. My father built a scaled down version of a wooden china cabinet for us. It even had glass in the doors that opened. He made a matching table and two child sized chairs, perfect for tea parties and playing house. My father did such a fine job on the wooden furniture. The pieces were finished so perfectly, they looked like they were bought from a toy store.

My parents had great friends, Bill and Etta Burkett, who lived beyond Aunt Jean's house. They had children named Bill, Evelyn, and Bobby. Evelyn was a year older than me and her nickname was "Teddy." She and I were the very best of friends. We played together growing up and remained friends all through our lives. Teddy's father made her the very same table, chairs, and china cabinet that my father had made for me. We had great fun using our imaginations as we played.

My father's older sister, Cecilia, her husband, Frank Zygmunt and their children had a large, beautiful home in Braddock. My father was close to Aunt Ceil, and always felt he could turn to her. He took his baby to her after his wife, Anna, died. Aunt Ceil was always there to offer emotional support to my father. I'll always remember her for her kindness, thoughtfulness, and hospitality. When my father was working and we would be off from school, my mother would take us by streetcar to visit Braddock. We would walk around, look in the stores, then get a hot dog and a frosty glass mug of cold root beer at the lunch counter at the Five and Ten Cent Store. We would walk down Second Street to visit Aunt Ceil, as her home was on the corner of Talbot Avenue. Even though we just had lunch, Aunt Ceil would insist on us having a cold drink and a cookie or piece of cake. When it was time to go home, Aunt Ceil would walk with us up Second Street, to the corner of Braddock Avenue, where we would get the number 55 streetcar back to Turtle Creek. She would wait with us until the streetcar came and then wave as we rode away. Aunt Ceil's home was the hub of social activity in the Krzyzosiak family and many special events and holidays were shared there. We were always welcomed at her house and enjoyed visiting and playing with our cousins.

Our home at 612 Locust Street in 1924.

Sometimes, my father would drive us to Braddock. We would shop and then visit Aunt Ceil and Uncle Frank. If the weather was nice, we would play outside on the big front porch, while my mother and Aunt Ceil would sit on a big swing. My father and Uncle Frank would make up an excuse to walk down for some "liquid refreshments", to a place on Third Street where they could enjoy some time for conversation to themselves. They would always return happy and smiling. Uncle Frank was a very smart man and was a printer by trade. He was also a brilliant musician and could play the organ and piano beautifully. Uncle Frank was my godfather and my grandmother was my godmother. We always looked forward to visits at Aunt Ceil's house.

We would occasionally go to visit my father's sister, Victoria and her children. They also lived in Braddock, on a very steep hill on Summit Street. After Aunt Vic lost her husband in the accident at the steel mill, she had a very difficult life and struggled to raise her children. She kept a spotless home and worked very hard. I especially remember she made the best, most delicious home-made vegetable soup with meatballs. She would always have a big pot of it cooking on her stove, and would insist that we have some soup with them. In later years, after all of her children were older, she worked at the lunch counter at the Sun Drug Store on Braddock Avenue, next to the bank. On shopping trips to Braddock, we would stop at the lunch counter for ice cream, if my Aunt Vic was working.

My mother told me about the time that we were driving home from Braddock on a dark, cold night. I was very small. It was raining. The rain was coming down harder and harder, and starting to mix with snow, as we drove on toward home. I was sitting on her lap in the front seat of the car, cuddled in a blanket to keep warm. I was getting restless and she was getting frightened, as they could hardly see in front of them. The roads were getting quite slick. My mother placed my little hand with hers, on the lever that worked the manual windshield wipers. She and I helped my father, by "working" the wipers, to keep the windshield clear. That occupied me and calmed her until we made it home safely.

As I got a little bit older, my cousin, Sylvia from Braddock would come and stay at our house. She was one of Aunt Ceil's daughters, and was about a year younger than me. We got along and played together very well. Sylvia and I were always very close to each other and remain so all through our lives. Sometimes, she would stay for a few days or a weekend, during the school year, but during the summer months, she stayed longer. Sylvia was quite young when she started to stay with us. I remember my mother used to tell her, "You can come and stay, but you can't wet the bed."

We would all go to the fields and meadows at the very top of the hill, beyond the pond, and pick violets and blossoms from the fruit trees. There was another wildflower that grew there that had white lacy blooms that were about five inches across. When we took the wildflowers to my mother, she would put a few drops of food coloring in a bowl of water. We would tint them before putting the flowers into a vase of water. They looked so pretty tinted and mixed with white flowers in a bouquet.

My parents, Irene, and me on Easter of 1927.

Later, in the summer, there would be elderberries, blackberries and strawberries to pick. My mother would give us each a pail and pack a little lunch. Then off we would go berry picking. Sometimes cousins would join us, also prepared with a pail and their lunches. We would go into the woods and fields and pick berries, and then enjoy the picnic lunch that our mothers made us, pick more berries, then make our way home. There was never a worry about us being safe. We would bring the berries home for my mother to make home-made jelly or jam. It was so delicious!

When I was three years old, we went on a picnic that was held by a lodge my father belonged to at the Sugar Camp picnic grove. It was out in Patton Township, north of the town called Pitcairn. My mother packed the picnic basket and we drove there in my father's car. It started out being a nice day, but then it rained in the afternoon. We got wet from the rain, and then suddenly it turned much cooler. In the next few days, I developed a cold and a sore throat, and I continued to get worse. I became very ill. My parents were very worried and sent for Dr. Morton. He came to the house, and gave me some medicine. My condition continued to worsen. I don't remember much from this time, but do remember being very sick. The doctor came back a few more times, tried different medicines, and nothing worked. I had diphtheria and the house was placed under quarantine.

At the time, there were outbreaks of illness or diseases and many of them were contagious. If someone in your house had one of the illnesses, a quarantine sign was placed on the front door. No one in the house could leave for the length of the quarantine. Signs were different colors for the different illness. This was not uncommon for quarantines to be issued for measles, mumps, chicken pox, scarlet fever and polio. If you were in school and had a brother or sister with one of these illnesses, you had to stay home. However, the school sent your work home, so you could stay caught up with your class. Well, Irene was thrilled.

I continued to get worse. At one point, the priest from St. Colman's Church came to give me last rites. Mrs. Chase, a neighbor who lived behind my grandmother's home, strongly believed in home remedies. She brought much of this knowledge with her from Italy. Mrs. Chase came to my parents' home and tried one of her home remedies to break my fever. It worked. My fever broke, though I was very weak and jaundiced. Thank goodness for Mrs. Chase and her home remedy, as I made a full recovery.

A local dentist, Dr. Alex Allan heard that I had been very sick. Dr. Allan practiced in Turtle Creek for many years, eventually becoming the school dentist, when a dental program was instituted for the students. He came to our door with the cutest little terrier dog, named Buttons. He told my parents he was trying to find a good home for the dog and thought I might enjoy having a dog. We were all excited and this really lifted my spirits. Buttons was fine for the first few days with us and Irene and I enjoyed playing with him. He was just adorable. Then, he started to cry and become very unhappy as he missed the Allan children. So Buttons returned home. I didn't have another dog until I was married. My parents had a dog named Dukie when they first moved into the house. Irene was small and she liked him a lot. For some unknown reason to me, Dukie died. They buried him in the backyard. Irene missed him and would look up at the moon in the night sky, point and say "Dukie." My parents told her that he went to heaven and she knew exactly where he was.

My father and me in 1928, while I was recovering from diphtheria.

We had two pretty little canaries. They were yellow and one of them had a little touch of black on the tips of its wings. They were kept in a cage in the dining room by the back window. Dickey and Suzie could sing beautifully. My father got them from Mrs. Decker, who lived in Cavittsville; a little town beyond Trafford. My parents had an old 78 record from Hartz Mountain that we would play and it would entice the canaries to sing. It really worked as they would sing along to the record. We had Dickey and Suzie for a few years and enjoyed them as pets.

Once, my father had gone by street car to a lodge meeting at the Polish club in Braddock. When he didn't return when expected, my mother was getting very worried. All of a sudden, a taxi pulled up in front of the house. My father got out and came up the walk to the front door. He had something hidden in his overcoat. It was a small, baby piglet. He won it in a raffle at the lodge meeting. The piglet was so cute and would squeak and cry, just like a little baby. My mother didn't want to keep it, so she gave it to my grandparents. It became a pet and followed my grandfather all over the yard. When my grandfather would sit on the swing on the back porch, he would call, "here, Piggy" and the pig would come and lay down at his feet. It would lay there for hours, while my grandfather rubbed the piggy's belly with a long switch. The pig kept getting bigger and bigger until it had to go somewhere else to live. They gave Piggy to Uncle Andrew whose family that had a big farm at Bear Rocks, near Seven Springs. When Piggy was slaughtered, no one in the entire family would eat any of the meat.

One time, my father tried to teach my mother how to drive the car. He took us up to a field behind my Uncle Charlie's house. Irene and I were still small. We were sitting in the back seat. My mother was actually doing a pretty good job for her first attempt at driving. All of a sudden, my father said something to her. My mother opened the car door and jumped out while we were still moving. Luckily, my father was in the front seat and was able to move quickly and stop the car. It's a good thing the car was not moving fast, as it was heading directly toward a pear tree. There could have been a serious accident. We met my mother back at the house and her driving lesson was never mentioned again. Although Jean and Dorothy were the only girls in my mother's family to have driver's licenses, they seldom drove.

I remember sitting on a stool watching my father repair the holes of the inner tubes of tires. He would use a patching kit which had rubber patches and adhesive glue. He would apply the patch and let it dry. Then, he would blow up the inner tube and submerse it in a wash tub of water or in the stationary laundry tubs in the basement. A leak showed bubbles when the tube was held under the water. If my father didn't see any bubbles, the hole was patched.

Just about every day, my mother would think of something that she needed from the store. My parents would usually go to Orr's Store which was located a short distance down Locust Street by the elementary school. However, on occasion, my mother would ask us to go to Straw's Store, which was located on the way down into Turtle Creek, on Maple Avenue. It didn't matter what the weather was like, my mother would say the walk was good for our health. As we got older, the errands led us into Turtle Creek. Irene, who was five years older than me, was sent on those errands alone. Usually the errands included going to the bank, and paying utility bills. One particular time, when Irene was about 11 years old, she was sent into Turtle Creek. Snow was falling. It was very cold and icy and beginning to get dark. As Irene was on her way home, a car skidded at the intersection of Grant Street and Maple Avenue. The driver didn't even see her, as her coat got caught on the bumper of his car and he hit her. There was a knock at the door and my mother opened the door. A stranger had Irene in his arms. She was not seriously injured. She had a few cuts and bruises, but she was absolutely scared to death. Thank goodness, her heavy winter coat had protected her. After that, the errands into Turtle Creek alone were absolutely forbidden by my father.

My father, Uncle Joe, and Uncle Charlie would go down into East Liberty in Pittsburgh, every once in awhile on Saturday mornings. Located there was the huge factory of the National Biscuit Company. They would go there and buy the day-old baked goods at nearly give-a-way prices and each would come back with a large bag full of things that cost all of 50 cents.

Oleo margarine would come in one pound blocks, or three pound tubs. To make it look more appetizing, it came with a packet of yellow coloring. We would mix it all in and it would look like butter, but it still didn't taste like butter. My parents would treat themselves once in a while and buy butter from the egg lady.

It was almost a necessity to go to the store often, as there were no freezers. Dry groceries and canned goods were always well stocked. In some areas, there still was no milk delivery, so we needed to go to the store regularly for milk, meats and cheeses. I do remember although I was very small, there was an icebox in the kitchen. The iceman would come every other day with a huge block of ice. He would carry the big block of ice, using a heavy metal device with prongs, and rest the block of ice on a large burlap sack that he had across his shoulders. He had to be strong to carry the block of ice all the way from his truck into the kitchen. The icebox was very well insulated. It had a pan underneath it to catch the water from the melting ice. My mother had to remember to empty the pan or she would have a real mess. When my mother got her first electric Westinghouse refrigerator, I was very young. It was a real luxury which pleased her immensely. The refrigerator sat up off the floor on little legs. It had no freezer section, but there was a compartment which held two metal trays for making ice cubes. The new refrigerator was helpful, but around the holidays, or on special occasions, it was just not big enough. My father constructed a window box for my mother to give her more cold storage space for food. The box was made from wood and lined with sheet metal. The window box worked very well in the winter as it was bitter cold and snowed. It was up on the roof of the covered back porch, so no animals would get into it. It was also more exposed to the wind there which kept the box even colder. From the back bedroom window on the second floor, we could easily open the lid, reach inside and get what we needed. It was very helpful.

My mother knew how to make soap. She was taught the recipe from an old farm lady. Everyone would save the used grease for her. When my mother had enough, she would melt it, then strain it to remove the impurities. I don't remember all of the ingredients, but I know it had borax and a touch of lye. As it would harden into large blocks, it turned very white. Then she would break it up into big squares. When it was time to wash a load of white clothes, my mother would grate some into the tub of the wringer washer. It was amazing the clothes didn't disintegrate, as it was very potent stuff. My mother never needed bleach.

My parents in 1929.

At the end of summer, it was canning season and time to make jelly. Everyone helped. My mother would put the oil cloth on the kitchen table. Irene and I washed the jars in water, using a bottle brush. We dried them and set them upside on the oil cloth, to dry further. My mother and father would prepare the fruit and cook it on the stove. They would fill the jars with the jelly or preserves, and let it sit for a little while. Next, they would pour melted paraffin wax on top and put the lids on. The wax would create a seal so no air could get in to spoil the jelly or preserves. We always had several jars on hand. My grandmother and aunts would sometimes exchange jars, so everyone had a variety. My mother did the canning of vegetables very much the same sort of way. She also made catsup and chili-sauce, bottle the sauces and then cap them.

They were absolutely delicious! The other vegetables were put up in glass, quart-sized Mason jars. There would be bread and butter pickles, relish and piccalilli, also tomatoes, tomato sauce and green beans. They would also make peach butter. In the back of the concrete basement was a large storage room that went underneath the back porch. It was always cool down there, even in the heat of summer. My father built an entire wall of wooden shelves from floor to ceiling. This is where all of the canned goods and jellies were stored. It was also an ideal place to store baskets of apples and potatoes. Canning season meant quite a busy time at our house, and a lot of work. The aroma from my mother's kitchen was just incredible. All of the surrounding neighbors knew exactly what she was doing.

When the home-grown tomatoes were in season, they were so delicious, especially the beefsteak variety. They were gigantic. One of the best summertime suppers that I remember was a tomato sandwich. We would take two slices of fresh baked bread, spread them with butter and then add a nice, thick slice of tomato. It was an incredible sandwich and not very costly.

My father made home-made root beer. We always looked forward to when he made some, as it was so delicious. After the bottles were washed, filled and capped, we carried them from the basement to the backyard. We would lay the bottles on their side in the grass and turn them every day. When bubbles started to appear, we would take them back to the basement where it was cooler. If the caps were not put on correctly, as it would ferment, it could explode or the root beer would spoil. My father had great success with capping the bottles, so root beer was always so tasty.

"A family that does things together stays together" or so my mother always said. There was certainly a lot of togetherness at our house especially when it came time to scrub down the kitchen. My mother insisted on a pure, white kitchen, as it would always look so clean. Keep in mind that most houses at the time had coal heat, including ours. If my father happened to be working that day, my mother handled the task just the same with her little helpers, Irene and me. She was a firm believer in a spotlessly clean house and a kitchen that was absolutely sanitized. My father or mother would stand on the top step of a wooden ladder and start with scrubbing the ceiling, first. From there, they would start working part way down the walls. Irene was five years older than me and taller. She would take over from where my parents left off. I would stand on a box and take over from where Irene left off, and clean all the way down to and including the baseboards. I don't think I necessarily did a great job scrubbing, but my parents could keep an eye on me. It taught me about housekeeping and how to work hard. During the cold months when the furnace was used, we would do the scrubbing once a month. Once the furnace wasn't used, we would do the kitchen scrubbing every other month. We enjoyed the reprieve.

When Irene and I were done with the chores, we would ask if we could go out to play. My mother would say, "First, go and see if your grandmother needs your help." So, we would go and see if she wanted us to help her. Another of my mother's famous sayings was "Busy hands are happy hands." and those hands never got into any trouble.

At the beginning of the Depression, things were really getting to be very bad. Irene and I were children and did not know what was going on. We never knew that people were poor, as our family and extended family were all in the same boat. No one sat and cried. We got up in the morning, listened to the radio and sang a song. After chores were done, we would go and play. People got up every day and did something. Even though times were getting very tough, people still looked for a little bit of pleasure. There was no such thing as public assistance, food stamps, welfare or unemployment compensation. What we had, we had and what we didn't have, we didn't. Families helped other family members and neighbors helped neighbors. The work at the Westinghouse plant slowed down. My father and the others who worked there were lucky if they worked two or three days a week. This meant a drastic reduction in income. My parents were not wasteful and managed to survive by using things wisely, even their income.

Right before the start of the holiday season, Irene and I walked with our father to the main gate of the Westinghouse plant, pulling our wagon. Food items were being distributed to the employees that were laid off or that were working with their hours cut back. You received a large sack of flour, a sack of sugar, a large sack of potatoes, a box of powdered milk, and a three pound tub of margarine. We loaded the items into our wagon and walked with my father as he pulled it back up the Electric Plan hill. These staples were greatly appreciated. I'm certain that many families that were affected by these difficult times were thankful.

With so many cousins of different ages and sizes, there was a great abundance of hand-me-downs that were usually in very good condition. Clothes were recycled among the families. I could count on getting a new dress for my birthday, Christmas, Easter, and the first day of school. That was something my mother insisted upon. We always started school with a brand new pair of shoes. My parents saw to it that we went to school dressed nicely.

When my mother purchased a twenty-five pound bag of flour, it came in a cloth sack. The sack was made with a printed, cotton cloth in a subtle pattern. After the flour was used, my mother would pull a thread and the cloth sack would separate into a nice piece of fabric. After the fabric was laundered, it was very soft. The fabric was used for making kitchen towels, aprons, nightshirts, blouses and skirts for the girls. My mother had a treadle sewing machine. Learning how to make kitchen towels was the first lesson in sewing for Irene and me. The flour sacks were actually not too bad. During those times, nothing went to waste. When I was a little older, my grandmother taught me how to do embroidery and I would do trim on pillowcases. My grandmother could embroider and crochet beautifully. She taught herself. She was a whiz at reading patterns and crochet directions. My grandmother taught me how to do a lace border on handkerchiefs. My mother also did beautiful hand work, so Irene and I had great teachers.

Uncle Joe's wife, Aunt Anne, taught us how to make beautiful flowers out of colored crepe paper and a piece of craft wire. She was very good at making the flowers and patient enough to teach us. Once we got the hang of it, they were easy to make. A bouquet of the crepe paper flowers was so pretty and colorful.

It was also quite popular at the time for women to make throw pillow covers with what was called a "yo-yo" pattern. We would cut round circles of fabric and finely stitch them together, on a plain pillow cover. It was as much work as quilting but the results were beautiful. It was a great wintertime project, as it took a long time to complete. It required many neat, little stitches, and fabric remnants left over from other sewing projects could be used. Not only were women skillful in crafts, but also resourceful with the materials.

Uncle Charlie, my mother's oldest brother was very civic minded. He felt compelled to help the people of Electric Plan, and Turtle Creek. He approached county officials about starting a depression garden and they agreed. The county sent men to plow and till the soil in the open fields at the top of Electric Plan just beyond the pond and the woods. The area was then staked off into forty-three plots of ground that were twenty five wide by one hundred feet deep. It cost fifty cents to register for a plot and that included the plants and seeds which were provided by the county. Sharing a plot was permitted but each person was required to register and share in the expenses. We were responsible for tending to our plot and keeping the plants healthy, free of insects, and well watered. Watering was done from a fresh spring which was close by that actually fed into the pond below. I was very young but remember my sister and I had tin cups to dip into a pail of water to help water the plants. We also weeded the garden, but my parents did the hoeing. The gardens helped to feed many hungry families and helped them to survive those tough times. Every plot was in use. Uncle Charlie acted as the overseer of the project and took care of the registration. The project went on for a couple of years. It taught people about agriculture and created not only a bond, but a very strong work ethic. The gardens were located where the Electric Heights Housing Project was completed in 1941. The housing project was built to accommodate the influx of workers and their families who came to work at the Westinghouse plant for the war effort.

One of the main lines of the Pennsylvania railroad ran right along Turtle Creek behind the Westinghouse plant. The tracks went between Philadelphia to the east and then directly into Pittsburgh, in the west, and beyond. During those times, many unfortunate men and boys would ride the rails, looking for work. They would walk through East Pittsburgh, Turtle Creek, and the other towns in the valley. On rare occasion, they would even find their way to the Electric Plan Hill and to our house. My parents never refused anyone. They would bashfully knock on the back kitchen door, asking if they could work for some food. My mother would ask them to wait quietly on the back porch steps. She would make them a couple of jelly or cheese sandwiches, wrapping them in wax paper. My mother would get them a drink and perhaps a cookie and a piece of fruit. She would hand the food to them graciously and say, "No one ever works for food at my house. Please sit and enjoy your meal." If my father was home, he would take them a big cup of hot coffee. He'd sit with them on the porch steps, smoke a cigarette and talk to them. They were always very polite and thanked my parents immensely. Somehow, they would mark our house. After weeks or even several months, it seemed like the same people would return, just as polite and as thankful as before.

If my father bought cigarettes from a store, he always smoked Camels. But most of the times, my mother would roll cigarettes for him. I remember my mother rolling cigarettes, using papers that she bought in a store. The tobacco came in a tin. She would put the paper in a small metal contraption that held it in place. Next, she would sprinkle tobacco onto the paper. My mother would turn a crank and out came a perfectly rolled cigarette. My father would keep them in a little cigarette case and in his smoking stand cabinet in the house.

In 1933, there was a terrible fire in Turtle Creek at the big school on Penn Avenue. The school was originally built in the 1890s, and most of it was destroyed. While the school was being rebuilt, portable buildings were put up in the playground area of our small Electric Plan Elementary School to help serve some of the students who were displaced. One of buildings was used as an all purpose room and often used for community events. I remember going to a neighborhood party there one evening with Irene and my parents. They had a round and square dance. Little children were welcome, if they stayed to the side and did not get in the way. I remember the music played and the people walked in a circle to the music. It was called a cake -walk. When the music stopped, the couple in the center of the room, under a big flag, won a cake. It was a wonderful night of entertainment and fun.

There were two classrooms in the basement of the school. In the evenings, one of the rooms was used for adult education. They would teach English to adults who were not fluent. The other room was used for training for the W.P.A., which was a government run program that gave people jobs. All of the students that lived below Albert Street on Electric Plan would attend the big school on Penn Avenue, in Turtle Creek. Students living above Albert Street and beyond into Patton Township, would attend the Electric Plan Elementary School. Every day, the janitor would go into the schoolyard and pull the rope on the huge bell which would ring the start of school in the morning. He would do the same for the afternoon session. The school bell could be heard for miles.

We always enjoyed school and then it was so much more stimulating than just studying to take tests. The teachers worked hard to keep it interesting and fun. They truly cared about the students. By the time you finished the sixth grade, you knew addition, subtraction, division, and multiplication. We learned how to make change with money. We learned fractions and the Roman numerals. We were not taught these skills using calculators or computers. Above and beyond the formal education, we were taught to get along with others, among many other social skills.

Before we started school, my mother taught us the entire alphabet. We learned how to write the letters and our name. We could count to one hundred, knew our address and colors. She was a very diligent teacher. My mother taught us nursery rhymes and songs. Keep in mind that there was no such thing as kindergarten or pre-school. We went directly into first grade and there was no turning back. It was a mother's important responsibility and job to help form her child's character during the early years. It made us who we are and I'm certainly very proud of it. There were so many happy memories of those early years at home with my dear mother. We had a lot of fun together.

As Irene was older than me, I got to watch her go off to school first. She was definitely a sassy, little girl. She would often get in trouble because of things she would say and how she would say them. One day, she got a little smart with her teacher, Mrs. Plotner. The teacher said she was going to give her a smack with the paddle for being sassy. Irene told Mrs. Plotner, "Go right ahead and do it because my mother is big and fat and she'll come right down here and sit on you. You'll get squished for sure!" Well, Irene avoided a paddling that day, but had to bring home a note to my mother in a sealed envelope. When Mrs. Plotner would see Irene or my mother in later years, the recollection of the incident would always bring smiles to their faces.

My parents always told us that "if you ever get into trouble at school or with your teacher, you'll be in bigger trouble, once you get home." On another occasion, my sister was told to go into the cloakroom at the back of the classroom and wait there for punishment, which meant the paddle. She and the boy next to her were standing at the blackboard talking, during an arithmetic problem. They went into the cloakroom as they were told but then Irene climbed out of the window and ran home.

There were children then, as there are now, who were slow to learn and very disruptive to the rest of the class. They needed firm discipline and special attention to be taught the most basic of skills and knowledge. These children were placed, in what was known as the "opportunity room." The teacher would teach them using methods that were more "hands-on." I remember them weaving big braided carpets, made out of cloth scraps on a type of loom. It would teach the children counting skills and how to follow instructions. They made other projects in there that helped them to learn. It was a unique way to teach the basic skills that the rest of us that were more disciplined could learn in a regular classroom. I knew some of the children who were in the opportunity room and they went on to have very productive lives. A few of them had their own businesses.

The neighborhood schools were so nice. Not only did we get to know the teachers and the teachers get to know us, they also knew all of our families. They knew my parents and my cousins and their parents. Everyone looked out for one another and helped each other out. The teachers had quite a job. When it was winter, the teacher had to help the little children with their boots and make sure that they were bundled up before going outdoors. Everyone at the Electric Plan Elementary School went home at lunch time, regardless of how far it was. This was a neighborhood school and there was no lunch room. Coats, boots and galoshes were kept in the cloakroom that was at the back of the classroom. The cloakroom was also a place of punishment as well. Most of the teachers were graduates of a two year teachers college or what was referred to as "normal school".

There were always holiday parties in the classroom in those days. Parents and teachers contributed their time and effort and home-made treats. My mother would send decorated cupcakes, marshmallow snowmen, cut-out sugar cookies and little flower pots with flowers made from gum drops. Everyone was always amazed at my mother's talents and creations. At Halloween, we could wear a costume to school. The teachers would have a Halloween parade around the outside of the school. Costumes were not store bought but made from things at home. We would be a witch, a princess, a hobo, or a ghost. Things and ideas were simpler and required creativity. Every day, when we were at school, we were given a half pint of milk at recess. The teacher would also pass out crackers. Milk and crackers were provided at no charge. They wanted to insure the students had good nutrition.

We did not have a great abundance of toys or games. We had dolls, a doll carriage, paper dolls, a china tea set, and a few games. We were happy using our imaginations and we would entertain ourselves for hours. My favorite doll was my Shirley Temple doll. I got her at Christmas one year from Santa. I'm certain that she was an extravagance for my parents. My Shirley Temple doll came with a fur coat and muff and she was wearing a matching little beret hat. I just loved her and she was one of my prized possessions.

In the winter, when we could not play outdoors, we kept ourselves busy with our toys and games. Sometimes, we would put up the card table and put a blanket over it. It would become many things and it would keep us busy for hours. Sometimes, it was a playhouse or it was an Indian tent or a secret hideaway or even an Army fort depending on who you were playing with and what your imagination conjured up in that moment. Even without television, there was no shortage of ideas that kept us entertained and out of our mother's way.

We enjoyed playing Checkers, Jacks, and our favorite game was Parcheesi. When I was very young, we would play a game called "Button, Button, Who's Got the Button?" In nice weather, we would play hopscotch. My father also made us little toys. He used to take a wooden spool from thread and cut notches in the edges of it with a pen knife, creating little teeth. He would make a small washer out of wax and place it over a hole on one side with a wide rubber band through it and the spool. We would either use a matchstick or a nub from a pencil in the other side then would wind it up, put it on the floor and release it. The spool would take off across the floor until it wound down.

When we were a little older, my mother taught us some card games. We would play Fish, Old Maid, and 500 Rummy. Some of the cousins and my friends liked to come to our house to play cards. The rule was homework had to be done first and they could not come on school nights. They always knew that my mother would have a freshly made treat. Their favorite was devil's food cake or oatmeal cookies. My friend Teddy told me "No one's mother makes treats as tasty, as your does."

There was one street lamp over on Cedar Avenue near Aunt Jean's house. We would go up there and play kick the can, roller skate, play catchers and hide-and-seek. We loved to jump rope and learned to Dutch jump. It was a lot of fun. We stayed in our own neighborhood and played with the cousins and with our little friends who lived close by. There were no such things as gangs except perhaps in the big cities. I'm sure that is why so many of my cousins like Sylvia from my father's side of the family loved to come and stay. Turtle Creek Borough had a curfew which was 9:45 at night. A whistle would sound from the fire department garage. It would echo and resonate up from the valley below, so it was easy to hear. Once the signal was heard, minor children had better start on their way home. An ordinance required minor children to be off the streets and home with their parents by 10:00 at night. Everyone obeyed without question.

There was not much money to spend, but no one really seemed to care about that at all. Everyone was in the same position and with a lot of young families tried to improvise and have fun. On Sunday afternoons, we would all read the "funnies" from the newspaper with my father. We would spread them out on the floor in the living room. We enjoyed reading about the escapades of Popeye and Olive Oyl, Tillie the Toiler, Katzenjammer Kids, Maggie and Jiggs, and of course, Orphan Annie.

The radio in our house was on most of the time as my parents, like their parents, loved music. My father was very proud to own a beautiful Atwater Kent console style radio that actually had a short-wave band. We could get broadcasts from all over the world. It was very interesting and entertaining. I remember at midnight on one station from Australia, the kookaburra bird call would signal the time. The radio had many good programs other than just music. We always enjoyed George Burns and Gracie Allen, Amos and Andy, and Little Orphan Annie. Irene and I never missed Little Orphan Annie. Like every other child that followed Annie and her dog Sandy, I had the decoder ring. At the end of each broadcast, a secret message was given to the listeners to decode on their rings. It was fun and it kept you as a faithful listener. Many years later, that radio became obsolete. My father disassembled the cabinet as it was just beautiful. It had been replaced by another console radio with a phonograph. My father carefully removed the beautiful cabinet top and attached the legs from the bottom of the cabinet. It made a beautiful pier table that I still have in one of my bedrooms. It brings back so many memories. Years later, Irene's youngest boy, Joey snuck out of the house one day and took the table up to Aunt Betty. He offered to sell it to her for 50 cents. Joey certainly got on my mother's bad list that day!

Across from our backyard, there was a vacant lot and then another house which my father built for the Gorazd family. The boy cousins would go over to the vacant lot and dig a big hole, a few feet deep. They would get twigs, paper, and other kindling, and sometimes even pieces of coal from home. They built a fire in the hole and we would meet them there with a raw potato from home. We would bury them on top of the fire and roast them. The boys were always in charge of the campfire. Sometimes, we would bring large marshmallows and toast them on long sticks over the top of the campfire. It was a lot of fun. When the potatoes were cooked, they were absolutely delicious even with the dirt and ash that covered them. We would eat them, skin and all. It just proves the point that eating a little dirt didn't hurt anyone. At the time of this writing, a few of us that ate those potatoes, are alive and doing well, including me. Imagine too, the children played with matches, didn't get burned, or set anything on fire that shouldn't have been. No one was poked in the eye with the sticks, as we toasted marshmallows. The freedoms of our childhood were priceless. Even at such young ages, we were taught the importance of the freedoms, and to respect them and not to abuse them. We certainly enjoyed them.

My grandfather went by train to visit one of his sisters. He had not seen her in a very long time and was excited to visit her. He did not stay as long as he had planned. When he arrived at her home, he was very disappointed by the fact that they were drinking. He went home as he missed being away from his family. The extra money he had saved to spend on his trip, he still had in his pocket. So he decided he would spend it on a summer party for all the children and grandchildren. We made home-made ice cream with my grandmother's churn. It was a big round wooden tub, and inside was a smaller metal tub, where the churn was, and where you would mix the ice cream. We would pack ice between the tubs, add the cream to the metal tub, and turn the handle. We all took turns and it was so delicious.

Once, lightening struck my grandparents' cherry tree in the backyard. It was loaded with fresh cherries. The next day, all of us gathered again to pick the cherries before the birds would eat them. We all had little metal pails and started gathering cherries from the tree that was now lying on the ground. We split the cherries and removed the stone. My grandmother made ice cream and put the fresh cherries in it. The tree was cut up for firewood, and a new fruit tree was planted in its place.

My grandparents' summer party in 1929.

There was an ash alley above the side of Uncle Charlie's house which went down between our backyard and the vacant lot. It continued down all the way to the concrete wall at the playground at the elementary school. When it would snow, this was the perfect place for sled riding. Someone would stand down where the alley crossed Larch Street near the school, to watch for cars. It was a nice ride and we had a good time. Some of the older kids were more adventurous and would ride down Locust Street, Maple Avenue, and continue down Grant Street into Turtle Creek. At the time, there were no slacks for girls to wear in the cold, snowy weather. The older girls wore heavy wool knee socks. The younger kids had snow suits that were so padded and insulated, they could hardly move.

I remember the boys wearing boots, called Ranger boots. The boots were brown leather, and had a pocket with a snap on one side. The big secret was that inside of the pocket was a Ranger pen knife. I guess it could be used for survival purposes while they were on the way home from school or the store. The real secret was the knife was so dull, it wouldn't even cut butter. The next rage with the boys was the aviator cap with the goggles. The boys went for the silliest of things. I'm sure those things boosted their egos and made their lives complete. None of them were ever sent home from school, suspended or expelled for wearing the Ranger boots.

In the summer, on the playground at the elementary school was an activity program every year. The older children would go and help teach the younger children games, crafts, and other activities. Irene and I would go and we really had fun. One summer, I remember making a necklace out of macaroni. We painted the macaroni first. When they were dry, we threaded them onto a string. The gym teacher was there to play baseball with the older boys and there was always a game of horseshoes going on. Of course, there were swings, a sliding board, and see-saws. There were picnic tables where we did the crafts and played games. The summer activity programs were sponsored by the community and the school. When we attended them, there was no fee. The programs continued through the years, as they were such a success and the children enjoyed them. My children attended and enjoyed the same summer activity programs as I did.

Air conditioning was completely unheard of in homes at that time. On hot summer nights, sometimes Irene and I took an old quilt and pillows and went to Aunt Jean's big front porch. We would sleep there with some of the cousins. We would take a flashlight and a bag of snacks. If we were not going to a sleep-out, we would have a sleep-out on our back porch. Not much sleeping was done, as we would tell stories into the night. No one ever had to worry about us and being safe outside. This was another freedom of our childhood and of the times.

Good people make a good neighborhood. Back doors were seldom locked, and if for some reason they were, everyone knew the spare key was under the mat. Growing up, we never heard of a robbery, even in those desperate times. Now, things have changed in every town. People have moved on and passed away. With the demise of the older generations, those values and quality of lifestyle are gone forever. There are a few older families left in Turtle Creek that still have familiar names. Time marches on.

When there was a suitable movie for children at the Olympic Theatre in Turtle Creek, Irene would take me. Some of the other, older cousins would also take their younger sisters and brothers. Starting at 12:30 pm on Saturday, the Olympic would have a children's matinee, featuring cartoons and a double feature. Usually one of the movies was a cowboy movie, and all of us liked that. As we would miss lunch, our mother would pack a good variety of snacks. We would always trade snacks with each other. Ray Figulski had the biggest bag with the most delicious assortment of snacks. The cost of the matinee wasn't very much and it kept us entertained all afternoon. If one of our parents didn't meet us with a ride home, it was a long walk back up the hill to Electric Plan. We always behaved when we were away from home and our parents. We knew better.

Jean Ross, who often played with us, was the same age as Irene. Jean lived in a little bungalow style house, across Cedar Avenue from Aunt Jean's house. Her Uncle Joe retired from many years in the Navy, and came to live with her family. He had a very nice, big car and we would all pile into the backseat. He would drive to the creek in Linhart, where he would park under a large shade tree. He would wash and polish his car in the shade, while all of us would go wading in the creek. It was a cool treat, during a hot summer day. Jean and I remained friends for the rest of our lives. In later years, we both worked at Gimbels.

In the summer months, one could also expect an occasional visit from the waffle man. He would park his vehicle on Cedar Avenue by Uncle Charlie's house. It was a truck that had been painted to resemble a circus wagon. It was very colorful. The back of it had a self contained kitchen with a window at the rear. There was a metal triangle that he would ring to announce his arrival. He always had a couple of women with him to help make the waffles. The waffles came plain or sprinkled with powdered sugar or with ice cream between them, like an ice cream sandwich. People from all over the neighborhood, would line up there. The lines would get long, if we didn't hurry when we heard him ring the triangle. I don't remember the cost of them, but I'm sure that they were only a few cents. The ice cream sandwich waffles were a real summertime treat.

In those days, it was very common to have people selling things come to the door. We had an egg lady that came to our house for many, many years. We would give her a bowl and she would fill it up with eggs. In fact, my kids remember her. We would also see hucksters of all types selling food such as fresh garden vegetables, bakery goods, and breads. I remember the umbrella man very well. He was an older man, rather slight, and spoke broken English. The umbrella man walked all over the hills and towns of western Pennsylvania. He had an apparatus strapped to his back which had a grinding wheel, and other various tools. Affixed to it was a bell that he would ring, as he walked, so you knew he was coming. He repaired umbrellas and sharpened knives, scissors, and razors. He also did other types of gadget repair.

The milkman from Valley Dairy started to deliver to us when I was very small. He would come a few times a week during the early morning hours, so the fresh milk would be there when we got up. If the weather was cold, the cream on the top of the milk would push the lid off. When we finished the glass bottle of milk, we would wash it out, and put it outside for the next delivery. He would pick up the empties and bring you full ones on his next trip. He would leave the bill every couple of weeks and then collect payment. Milk has never tasted as good. I think it was because of the glass bottles, and the lack of preservatives.

A wonderful Italian family built a beautiful, light brick home on the lot above ours. The bricks used to build the house were imported from Italy. Frank and Helen Palmer were excellent neighbors and had children about the same age as us. Many times, Frank would call my father over to let him sample the home-made Italian wine which he made in his basement. Some summer evenings, Mr. Palmer would sit on their back porch and play beautiful music on his accordion.

There was another old-fashioned, Italian family, the Lauritos who had a huge house at the corner of the playground on Locust Street. The Lauritos had seventeen children. They had spring water well in the backyard and a big old fashioned pump on the back porch. Mrs. Laurito would let you pump it yourself. The water was always so ice cold, even in the heat of summer. The Lauritos were such a nice family. Some of the children were from Mr. Laurito's first wife that had passed away. They kept a cow for fresh milk. Very early every morning, one of the boys or Mr. Laurito would take the cow up the ash alley at the end of our backyard. They would take her to a field at the top of the hill by the depression gardens. With a very long rope, they would tie her to a tree and leave her a wash tub with water. She would graze up there all day and no one would bother her. Just before dark, someone would bring her back down for the night. As the neighborhood grew and zoning codes changed, shortly after World War II, the cow had to be moved to a farm.

Turtle Creek was really a melting pot of people and families of various ethnic backgrounds including the English, Scottish, Irish, Eastern Europeans, and Italians. Our immediate neighbors were mostly Eastern Europeans and Italians. An Italian family purchased a lot and built a house between my grandparents' house and Aunt Jean's and Uncle Andy's house. When one of the daughters was married with a large church wedding, there was a reception at their home, even including an orchestra. After dark, all of us got metal pots or pie pans and wooden spoons. We all stood around their front porch and started beating the pots and pans. The noise was loud and the music paused. Out walked the beautiful bride and groom. It was their custom for us to do this and to give us colored Jordan almonds and Italian cookies.

One night, very late, my grandmother and the girls that were still living at home had quite a surprise. They were awakened by a terrible blast that shook the house and rattled the windows. Apparently, a neighbor had developed a bad relationship, or had bad business dealings with someone who was not so nice. Someone had thrown some dynamite down his chimney, and it exploded. It blew the brick chimney to pieces and put a very large hole in their roof, and down into the rest of the house. Nobody said a word, as everyone knew what happened and wanted to save them the embarrassment. The fortunate part was that no one was hurt. The house was empty while they repaired it and they eventually moved back in. Everyone in the neighborhood ignored it and life went on. Most of those neighbors were gracious enough not to ask questions and minded their own business.

My mother was a real magician in the kitchen even when money was very tight. She always made sure that we had a proper diet and good healthy meals. She always tried to buy extra food when she could to put away on the grocery shelves for later use. My father and mother both enjoyed their treats, as we all did. Every fall, we would make fudge and hand pulled taffy. Sometimes, the cousins would come and help pull the taffy. We would wait until it was just cool enough to pull. Then we put butter on our hands, so the taffy would not stick as we pulled it and worked it.

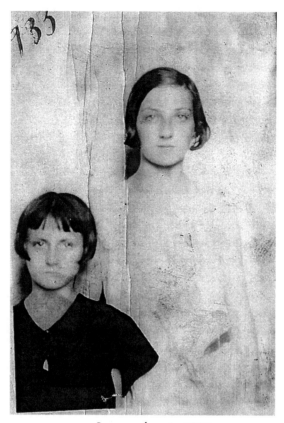

Irene and me in 1933.

At Halloween time, there was no shortage of home-made treats. My mother would make caramel corn and load it with cashew nuts and peanuts or sometimes she would form caramel popcorn balls. She would make peanut brittle and red candied apples. There were no electric popcorn makers, so we would pop the corn in a kettle on the stove or in a wire basket in the fireplace.

Birthdays were always very special in our house. It was just like another holiday celebration. My father never had the luxury of celebrating his birthdays while he was growing up. So, he made certain that ours were well observed. Of course, at that time, money for extravagances or anything elaborate just wasn't there. My parents always saw to it that we got a birthday gift, a new dress, and had a party with cousins and friends invited. My mother would bake a special cake of her own creation. The cake is always referred to as "Aunt Helen's Merry-Go-Round Cake." She would bake two round layers of cake using yellow batter, which she would divide. She reserved a little of it in two little bowls. The rest of the batter would go into two round layer cake pans. The batter in the two bowls is tinted with food coloring. One was a shade of pink and the other one was in a shade of green or blue. Then, with the tip of a knife, she would swirl the colored batters into yellow batters. Once the cake was baked, she would frost and stack the layers with white frosting. She would place iced animal crackers in a circle on the top of the cake. Behind each animal, she would place a candy stick or peppermint stick to resemble the poles on a carousel. Then, if she really wanted to be creative, she would fashion a cone shaped top out of construction paper for the roof. When the cake is sliced, it looks like a rainbow. To have such cake on my birthday, was such a very special treat, as I knew just how much effort and time my mother put into making it. In my mother's memory, this cake is still made and enjoyed today.

The day after Thanksgiving was the official start of the Christmas season. My parents would bundle us up since the weather was usually cold and we would be off for downtown Pittsburgh. There was always a big Santa Claus parade. The holiday trimmed windows of the big department stores were unveiled and Santa was available to discuss wishes. After the parade, we would look at the windows. They were always so beautiful. I think the animated villages gave my father plenty of ideas for his own displays. We would then go inside of the stores, and look at the beautiful decorations. They were always so elaborate. Even with the times being what they were, my parents managed to somehow buy us each a pretty, new dress. We always went to lunch at McCrory's Five and Ten store. They had the best hot roast beef sandwiches and mashed potatoes with gravy. That is what we would usually get. It was such a treat! The tradition continued all through my childhood and into adulthood when we would do the same with our children.

One Christmas, my father was opening the branches on a beautiful evergreen tree that he had just purchased and he found a little glass bottle with a note inside. He gave the bottle to me and said "This must be for you." The note was written by a little girl about my age. The beautiful tree had come from her family's Christmas tree farm in Boiseton, New Brunswick. Her name was Marcilyn Farley. The note said she would be happy to know where the tree would be on Christmas Day and then she wished us a Merry Christmas. I was just amazed, so I wrote to her. We became pen-pals and corresponded for several years, then lost touch. The tree was such a special, beautiful Christmas tree.

In the Polish culture, Christmas Eve was called *Wilia* and was a very important event. It starts on Christmas Eve, when the first star appears in the night sky. A special, seven course dinner was served consisting of a mushroom soup, boiled potatoes with parsley, fish, pickled herring, pierogies, fried cabbage, winter vegetables, and home-made bread. We also had fresh baked cookies and nut roll. Everyone in the entire family and I mean everyone, came.

It would be a disgrace and an insult to the family and your heritage not to attend *Wilia*. All of the family would gather at the home of my grandparents. Over the years, as more marriages occurred, and more babies were born, the crowd attending *Wilia* grew and grew. The furniture had to be moved out of the first floor living room. The dining room table was opened up and extended with boards to go into the living room, making an extremely large table. Wooden folding chairs were borrowed from the church. Everyone brought food, helped to set the table, and helped grandmother prepare more food. An empty place was always set at the table for those in the family who had passed on, so they could be there in spirit and remembrance. It was a very festive celebration. After the meal, Santa would appear from the dark of the night. He would always have a huge cloth sack filled with a small gift and a peppermint stick for each child. As we got older, we noticed Santa smelled of a pipe or a cigar. Many of the men in the family enjoyed smoking pipes and cigars and I think we were getting wise. Once my grandfather died, the tradition of *Wilia* was passed on to the individual families. It was up to each family to have their own. Many in the family still follow the special celebration today.

Kolenda was another Polish custom followed on New Year's Day by our family. It would usually start with the head of the family or the oldest man in the family going to the house of the closest family member to wish him good luck and good health in the New Year. It would be done with a toast of liquor or whiskey in a shot glass. Along with the "snort", they would have a sweet or a slice of nut roll. Then the next man would accompany him to the next family's home where they would do the same. It was Uncle Andrew who got things started. First, they would go to all of the family homes, then to the homes of special friends. By the time they would be done, there were six or eight men or even more and they were all quite happy. I'm sure they went home for a nap afterwards. It was always customary to have a dark haired man be the first one to enter your home on New Year's Day. With him, came good luck in the New Year.

On the day before Lent every year, my mother would make Polish donuts called paczkis. They were raised, fried donuts with a fruit filling. She would fill some with lecvar or prune and some with apricot or cherries. Then my mother would roll them in granulated sugar. Paczkis were a lot of work to prepare but they were a Polish tradition on Shrove Tuesday.

My mother was known for was making another Polish donut called krusciki. She would make them for every holiday, baby shower, christening, wedding, or family party. My young cousin, Andy could probably smell the donuts when my mother was making them. Before she knew it, he would be at the kitchen door offering to help her. My mother would roll the dough out in wide stripes, cut a slit in the center and looped the dough in a knot. Then, she fried the donuts in hot grease in a cast iron skillet. When they were slightly cool, my mother would put them in a paper bag with powdered sugar and shake to coat them. That was Andy's job. He always came to our house to do that for my mother. She thought that was so special. My mother sent him home with a bag full of krusciki. I wonder how many of them were actually left when Andy got home.

Easter was another busy family holiday at our house. After church on Easter morning, we would have an egg hunt. My parents started cooking the day before. I remember them grinding horseradish roots with the old hand grinder and then blending the roots with grated beets which was eaten with ham or kielbasy. My mother baked a ham. We would have keilbasy and eat the colored eggs, Irene and I made. My mother always made a huge bowl of potato salad, some fresh baked bread, sweet bread, poppy seed rolls, and nut rolls, some with lecvar filling. The big table in the dining room would be set for a late lunch buffet and family would come and go all day long. I often wonder why no one ever got sick or got food poisoning as the delicious food was out all day long and sometimes into the early evening.

One day, my father came home and told us that a special surprise was coming. A couple of days later, a large truck pulled up directly in front of the house. My father bought a player piano. My mother wondered how he was ever going to pay for it. He told her not to worry as the man who owned it was desperate to sell it. My father bartered some construction work for the piano. It was a beautiful piano and came with a lot of music rolls. Irene and I took lessons from the nuns at St. Colman's for a few years. I hated the lessons so much my father said that I didn't have to go back. My sister and I continued to learn from a "Teach Yourself" book and ended up doing fairly well. My parents' favorite songs were "Bye Bye Black Bird", "Carolina Moon", "The Skaters Waltz", "Sail Along, Silvery Moon" and especially "Humoresque".

My father's Uncle Matthew, who lived on Fisk Street in Pittsburgh, came to visit along with his daughter Mary and her husband, Tom Pawlak. They played the piano, sang songs, danced and had a wonderful time. Uncle Matthew reached in his pocket and pulled out a large match box full of pennies. He sprinkled them in the back yard for us to play treasure hunt. Everything we found, we could use at the store to buy penny candy. It was such a big decision to make when you were standing at the store, selecting penny candy, piece by piece, from behind the glass counter. It was a lot of fun. I am sure the clerk couldn't wait for us to make up our minds and go home.

When I was very young, my parents took Irene and me to Braddock by trolley car. We heard there was going to be a Gypsy funeral procession for the king of the gypsy clan. He was a very good looking man and had long hair that he kept tied into a ponytail. I remember standing on the sidewalk watching the gypsies march by. My father had to lift me onto his shoulders so I could see as it was so crowded. The gypsy women and girls wore brightly colored skirts and blouses. Many carried flowers with colorful ribbons. There was a group of men, in front of the men carrying the coffin, playing violins and other musical instruments. A big flower arrangement in the shape of a violin was on his coffin, as he had played the violin. There was another group of musicians following behind the coffin. They all marched up the main street of the town and then to the Braddock Cemetery that was at the top of the hill. It didn't seem like a funeral as it was such a festive and colorful event.

My Uncle John was quite the character. As a career Navy man, his lifestyle was never too stable. He met and married Florence Wiggins, an Irish woman from Philadelphia. She had run away from a convent school and they met while he was stationed in California. His sisters were not very happy with his choice, as she tended to live life a bit on the wild side. Florence was not very attractive, but dressed stylishly and in the best of taste. She liked liquor and smoked cigarettes and on occasion, smoked a cigar or two. She was tattooed and was considered to be what was then known as a "flapper." Florence had a very flamboyant personality and could have a very harsh tongue. But she had a huge, loving heart. As most of John's family was not very accepting of her, my parents had open minds and hearts and enjoyed her company immensely. They never had children and were very close to us.

Uncle John and Aunt Florence would visit us often. She was very kind and always remembered Irene and me with some little gift. Every time they would come, it was like a party. The furniture in the living room was moved aside and the rug was rolled up. They would listen to music on the radio or play records or the piano. They would dance and sing into the night. Uncle John and Aunt Florence were very good dancers and knew the dances of the day. They loved to do the Charleston. It was so much fun to watch them and we all had a good time.

While on furlough from the Navy one time, Uncle John came to visit. The Ringling Brothers' Circus was going to be at Forbes Field, in the Oakland section of Pittsburgh. We were not going to be able to go to see it, but very early one morning, Uncle John took us down to the East Liberty train station and we watched the circus being unloaded from the train. It was a sight to watch all of the animals coming off the train and parading down the street. It was just like being at the circus and it didn't cost a cent. I remember how cute the elephants were, holding each other's tails by their trunks. Some of the clowns and other performers were also in costume and created a great circus parade. They marched all the way from the train station to Forbes Field. What a delight!

When Uncle John was in Japan, he sent beautiful silk kimono pajamas and matching parasol umbrellas for Irene and me. It was a lovely surprise. I remember how excited we were when the box arrived. He was very thoughtful.

Sometimes, a visit from Uncle John and Aunt Florence brought unexpected fun. Once, when they came they went to Braddock to visit one of his sisters, the tone of the discussion suddenly changed and harsh words started flying. An argument ensued. Aunt Florence was wearing a beautiful, black seal skin fur coat as the weather was cold and snowy. Suddenly someone gave Florence a shove, knocking her off balance. She sat directly on a lit gas burner and burned a hole in the seat of her fur coat! Aunt Florence took it off, threw the coat on the snow and started stomping on it to extinguish the fire. After all was said and done, Florence laughed about the whole incident.

We had a coal burning furnace and keeping it going was a real job. I remember my father going to the basement every night before bedtime to "bank" the furnace to keep the house warm all through the night. He would shake out the ashes with a long hooked rod and put in more coal. It provided very good heat, but it was so dusty. It's no wonder my mother wanted the kitchen scrubbed down so often. My father's brother, Edward, had my father build a house for him right next door on the lot below us. We had coal delivered at the same time as Uncle Ed. The truck would dump a large load of coal in the ash alley behind the houses. My father and Uncle Ed would use shovels to put the coal into wheelbarrows. Then they moved the coal to a little door on the side of the house. Behind the door was a chute which went into the coal bin and that is where my father would dump the coal. It was such a job! Eventually, Uncle Ed and my father installed coal cellars in the front of the house under the front porch. Then the truck could unload the coal right into the cellar using a chute from the front street. It wasn't until work picked up in the mid 1930's, that my parents could afford to install a gas-fired furnace. Thank goodness for that as the coal was so dirty and dusty.

There were no such things as automatic washers or dryers in those days. When we weren't in school, we would help my mother with the laundry. We had a Maytag wringer washer in the basement. Then, the laundry was carried out to the backyard and hung on a clothesline to dry. In the winter, laundry was hung in the basement or it would freeze solid. The heat from the coal furnace helped to dry them quickly. In the nice weather, the sheets and clothes smelled so clean and fresh when we would take them off the line. Irene and I would also help my mother with stretching the lace curtains on stretcher frames for drying once they were laundered. We had to be very careful of the tiny nails as they were very sharp and could prick our fingers. Once the beautiful curtains were dry, they hung so straight on the windows.

When Irene and I got a little older, we would help my mother with the ironing. She always had electric irons. An electric iron was one of the first things my grandmother got when electricity came to the Electric Plan in 1916. I'm certain that it was made by Westinghouse. There was a company store across from the main gate of the plant that sold Westinghouse products and appliances, offering employees special discounts and even time-payments. Every single article of clothing was ironed, including socks and underwear. My mother always told us "the heat from the iron sanitizes things and kills all of the germs. No one will ever get cooties or athletes foot." If we asked my mother a question as to why things were done, she would always have an answer. Some of her answers were very good ones.

Irene and I were taught all of our housekeeping skills from my mother and grandmother. We were taught to wash on Monday and iron on Tuesday. Windows were washed every Wednesday. We cleaned upstairs on Thursday and downstairs on Friday. Shopping was done on Saturday. Sunday was for worship and family. We never questioned the schedule and I still do things in this very same way today.

The ritual of spring cleaning was very important. We did this every year, whether it needed to be done or not. Usually, after winter with the dusty coal furnace, spring cleaning needed to be done. Walls were washed, wall paper was cleaned, and everything was washed and polished. There was no wall-to-wall carpet, so the room-sized carpets and area rugs were hung outside on the clothesline in the backyard. With a "carpet beater", we would literally beat and swat the dust out of them. I never understood this as we had a Bissell carpet sweeper and an electric vacuum cleaner that we used regularly. When we questioned my mother about this, she said, "Well, everyone does this to freshen things up and besides, do you want the neighbors to think we are dirty?" After all, we also didn't want to appear lazy. It was more than true, to say my mother was meticulous about housekeeping and our house. She would tell us "the Queen of England could ring our doorbell at eleven o'clock at night and I could let her in." Another of her famous sayings was "everything had a place and everything was in its place." Our house was always company ready and so was my mother.

Shortly before I was born, my father finished building a house for his youngest brother, Edward, who had purchased the lot next door and directly below ours on Locust Street. Uncle Eddie had been living in Braddock with his older sister, Ceil. Aunt Ceil was very busy raising a young family of her own. It was time for Eddie to get his own place and sister, Stacia would live with him. Uncle Eddie was legal guardian and in charge of Stacia.

She suffered from a head injury when she was a very young girl which left her developmentally disabled. As the story was told to us, Stacia fell out of a high window while she was chasing a canary that was loose in the house. The bird flew out the upstairs window and young Stacia followed after it. The fall caused some head injuries which resulted in child like behavior. She was quite capable of doing most things. But comically and sadly, she could be quite entertaining. Stacia would break into a silly song at the drop of a hat or speak in an odd mixture of English and Polish and sometimes, absolute gibberish. She was very sweet but was to be pitied. She and Uncle Eddie were dependent on each other and inseparable. Stacia would cook and help take care of the house and Uncle Eddie, in return would see to her care and give her a place to live. It was like living with a six year old in a woman's body. All through our early years and after, they lived next door. Aunt Stacia would always refer to my mother as "Mum," probably because she heard us call her that. Sometimes she had difficulty with names, but would just call you what she wanted. Aunt Stacia called me "Micky-Annie." From the side dining room window, we could look out and see a view through their kitchen window. As a treat, Uncle Eddie would bring Stacia a bag of peanuts. We would watch her as she would toss them in the air and catch the peanuts in her mouth. She would never miss. It wasn't uncommon that after dinner, she would let the dishes soak in the sink and then around midnight, she would wash them. Aunt Stacia created such a racket, as she banged the pots and pans as she washed them, while reciting mass in Polish or singing at the top of her lungs. One time, she decided to do laundry, long after midnight. We were awakened by a horrible scream. My father hurried, threw on some clothes, and ran next door. Aunt Stacia was in the basement doing laundry, alright, and her arm was stuck in the electric wringer on their Maytag washing machine. My father struggled to free her and finally did. They called the doctor who came to the house. Her arm was broken in several places.

Aunt Stacia would often come over and say, "Mum, let me help you," and start doing the dishes. She loved to help people and would visit the entire family and help them, too. It was not unlike her, to lift up her dress and get down on the floor, and play with us. She was a great playmate and a lot of fun. My children remember playing with her when they were small. Stacia ended up being the last survivor of the brothers and sisters. She lived to be well into her 90s. She died in an institution in the 1970s. She was a wonderful part of our colorful family and I'll always remember Stacia with love and compassion.

Uncle Eddie and my father ended up running the same machine in the micarta division, for Westinghouse Electric at the plant in Trafford, which was a little town further east along the Turtle Creek. My father would run the machine on the day shift and Uncle Eddie ran the machine on the third shift. My father took his lunch in a metal lunch container. When he would come home from work, we would always meet him at the back gate. He would give us his lunch container and we would proudly carry it into the kitchen. From his empty lunch container, my father managed to produce a little treat for us. I'm sure when my mother made his lunch, she made certain there was something extra in there for Irene and me. Once the grandchildren came, and he was still working, my father did the very same thing for them. Before he worked in Trafford, my father worked in the "I" building at Westinghouse in East Pittsburgh. There was a huge lay-off that affected him for quite a long while. He was eventually called back, but to the micarta division out in Trafford. My father told us that he would eat his lunch along the banks of the creek by the plant. Eventually, he made a little wooden stool to sit on as the banks along the creek were full of copperhead snakes.

It was probably late in 1935, before anyone noticed any improvement in the economy. By that time, all of the shifts were back to a normal schedule at the Westinghouse plant. Subtle signs of improvement were beginning to be apparent. Turtle Creek had grown into a great little town with many stores and shops lining both sides of Penn Avenue, the main street.

One of my mother's thrifty habits that stayed with me all though my life was stocking up the pantry. When my father was working regularly and there was a little extra money, the first thing that my mother did was to buy extra groceries to put away in the pantry. That way, we were always prepared for a tough time, should it occur or an emergency. There was also a rainy day fund, which was a little extra money that she would put away. After I got married, these practices got us through many labor strikes and lay-offs when my husband worked at Westinghouse. The longest one was five months long and that I'll never forget. If it wasn't for the rainy day fund, we would have been sunk.

It was by this time, that all of the rest of my mother's sisters were married except Edna. Irene married Gene D. Piazza, a nice, handsome man who also had a good job with Westinghouse. Dorothy married Albert Rapp. They had a simple ceremony and took a honeymoon cruise on the Great Lakes. Dorothy was very ambitious and worked in the office at Westinghouse. After work, she attended the Mason Felix Beauty School in downtown Pittsburgh. Dorothy loved doing hair and did all her sisters' hair. I still remember the scary electric permanent wave machine. In 1938, a short time after Dorothy was married, they purchased a large, beautiful home on old Route 22, out in the country, in Monroeville. The home had been converted to a tourist home, which they also operated. It was beautifully landscaped and had a large koi pond. It was known as Green Gables and was originally owned by a Packard dealer. We would visit her there and sometimes helped mow the grass with a power lawn mower. My mother would help mangle sheets for the guest rooms. Edna was the last girl to marry. In 1940, she married Steve Sikora. Steve, an amateur boxer, worked at Westinghouse. He once boxed with Billy Conn and Fritzy Zivic. As a young man, during the early thirties, Steve worked for the Civilian Conservation Corps or C.C.C., building roads and parks near Cook's Forest.

Turtle Creek experienced the "Great St. Patrick's Day Flood of 1936." A large area of downtown Pittsburgh was under water and the flooding continued up through the river valleys backing up into all of the small towns surrounding the rivers and Turtle Creek. This was not the first or last flood in Turtle Creek. Heavy rains caused a quick melt-down of snow which caused the rivers to swell beyond their size. History shows records of flooding in Turtle Creek in 1907, and in 1908. The flood in 1936 was quite major. The water ended going up Grant Street at the beginning of the Electric Plan hill. There was a lot of damage. In some places, the water was at least six feet deep. A few days later when the water receded, the massive clean-up began. The streets as well as once beautiful stores along Penn Avenue were covered with mud and debris. It was quite a mess. We were safe up on the Electric Plan hill but the Westinghouse plant was damaged. There was no electricity so we used candles for a few days. There was one casualty. A man, whose wife worked at Murphy's Five and Ten Cent Store, drowned. There were a few more major floods in 1954 and some minor ones in 1959 and 1960. Serious measures were taken by Allegheny County to implement a flood control project where gates were installed near the Westinghouse property, where Turtle Creek ran into the Monongahela River. If flooding started to occur down the river, the gates would be closed to protect the valley.

In 1937, my father purchased a new, green Willys automobile from Tony Caruso who was the Willys dealer on Ninth Street in Braddock. It was a very well made car. My father was so proud to own a brand new car. Times were starting to get better.

I was graduating from the eighth grade in 1939 and was very, very excited. There was going to be a ceremony, a party and a dance. All of the girls had to make their dresses. We started to make them months ahead of time. We used the same pattern, so we would all match. The fabric was a beautiful dotted Swiss and we could choose pink, light green, yellow, or light aqua. I chose yellow. The home economics teacher, Miss Findley, helped us cut the dresses out with the pattern. Mothers could help us pin them together, but we had to sew them on our own. It was part of our final grade. The dresses were ankle length with a long ribbon sash. In the class photo, we all looked so nice. The patterns and the material were ordered through the school at wholesale cost so the dress wasn't very costly to make. I enjoyed doing it and then wearing my dress to the festivities. We were all so proud of our accomplishments. The boys were required to wear sport jackets, white shirts and neck ties. Everyone looked so nice and we felt very grown up.

For my birthday that year, I could pick three friends. I chose Teddy Burkett, Ellie and Betty Bouma. My father drove us out by Greensburg and watched as we went ice skating. My mother sent along a Thermos jug of hot cocoa and home-made cookies. It was a nice birthday treat and we had such fun.

Sometime in the late thirties, my father took a two week vacation from Westinghouse. We went to see Uncle John in New Jersey. Uncle John and Aunt Florence wanted my father to do the framing on a house they were building in Pleasantville, which was right outside of Atlantic City. When we got there, the foundation was ready. My father, Uncle John, and Joe Wiggins, who was Aunt Florence's brother, had the framing up by the time we went home. All of us girls camped out in Uncle John's garage while they were working and we had a lot of fun.

One of my father's Navy friends had a big beautiful house on the Narragansett Bay in Newport, Rhode Island. The "Hurricane of 1938" went right through the area, causing great damage to sections of their roof and the widow's walk. My father drove up there to offer his assistance and carpentry skills. He spent about two weeks there helping them make repairs. They sent a gift home for my mother. It was a new Hamilton Beach stand mixer which she used until she passed away. With that mixer, my mother made many delicious treats.

Things in the world were changing and we were worried about family who lived in Poland. My father's older sister, Helena (Lena) married a Polish man. They were living in a town called Wilmerding, just east of Turtle Creek, where he worked in another Westinghouse factory that made air brakes for trains. His family owned a factory in Poland and his father was very ill. If his father had passed away, without a survivor to take over the house and family business, the government would confiscate everything. They moved back to Poland before World War I, settled and had a family. Everyone kept in touch with Lena and her family although miles away and separated by an ocean. It was a frightening time there, as a man named Hitler was getting to be very powerful.

Me in 1939, wearing the dress that I made for eighth grade graduation.

In 1939, Irene graduated from Turtle Creek Union High School. She got a job as a secretary for Ohringer's Furniture Store in Braddock. In 1940, she met and married John (Jack) Sapp whose family lived at the top of Pitcairn hill on Seventh Street. They eloped to Wellsburg, West Virginia, as it seemed to be the thing to do. Neither of the families were thrilled about their marriage. Jack's family was Presbyterian and he had the reputation of being a lady's man, which he definitely earned. Ohringer's sent a limousine to the house for Irene and my mother. As a wedding gift, Irene could go to the store and select whatever she wanted.

In 1940, Maria, one of the young cousins living in Poland was teaching school. The Nazis took occupation of the town in mid-September. She was cooking and taking food to captured prisoners of war who were kept in temporary housing nearby. Maria also helped a couple of these prisoners escape to the Polish Army in the west. On September 24, the Nazis came to the school where she was teaching and took her away. She wasn't permitted to say goodbye to her mother and family. The family thought she had been taken to jail. The Nazis took her to Tarnow first, then to Ravensbruck, but no one in her family knew where she was or what might have happened to her.

At that time, work at the Westinghouse plant was picking up tremendously. They were starting to work on government contracts. The contracts weren't for refrigerators or appliances, but for helmets, motors and military parts. It was a sure indicator of what was to come.

Things on Electric Plan were changing, too. At the very top of the hill where the depression gardens once were, a huge housing development called the Electric Heights Housing Project was being built. It was built for the people and their families who were moving into the valley to work at the Westinghouse plant. More people were needed to help with the work from the government contracts. The housing project officially opened for occupancy in 1941. It was a well planned community. During the building of the project, the demographics of Locust Street changed. The big pond was drained and filled in and the road was paved and connected to James Street that went out into Monroeville and Patton Township. Some of the woods were disappearing which made us sad but the Indian path was still there. It was then that a local bus company would start to make daily trips from Turtle Creek onto Locust Street and Electric Plan. It was a convenience that we all appreciated. The streets below Locust Street were also paved and connected to James Street. The streets were called Mercer and George. There was also an old settler's log cabin that was up in the woods along James Street which I remember quite well. We would often wonder who had lived there in years gone by. The cabin was destroyed by fire one night and gone forever.

The War Years
and Getting Married

I guess I really don't consider the Depression being over until about 1940. That's when things really turned around, right before the war started. A lot of families were still recovering from the Depression. Some had lost their homes, as well as their savings and investments. Some losses could not be replaced. Not many in my class had the means to go on to college as the Depression depleted the family's savings, if they even had any to deplete. Homes were in need of repair. Things that were wearing out needed to be replaced. It had been so long since anything that cost money could be done.

My father and Uncle Eddie would talk about all of the contract work for the government that was coming in. There were orders for helmets, mess kits, canteens, trays, and tables for the Army bases. I distinctly remember December 7, 1941, when Pearl Harbor was bombed and war was declared. President Roosevelt made the announcement on the radio; his voice was grave and serious. For many years, we listened to the famous fireside chats, but this was different.

Once the war started, so did the rationing. Books of ration stamps were picked up at the borough building in Turtle Creek. Stamps were used to purchase meat, butter, sugar, gasoline, and tires. The amount of gasoline given was based on the distance driven to the job. A lot of people joined "share-a-ride" programs and carpooled to their jobs, as did my father. He shared a ride with Mr. Piper from Locust Street and his friend, Granville Jones who lived by the Bellwood school. Most people bought retreaded tires as they were exempt from rationing. Irene left her job with Mr. Ohringer and went to work at the Westinghouse plant. The wages were not bad and families were able to live on those wages. It's a shame that it took the war to stimulate the economy into a more healthy state.

There were civil defense patrols in all of the neighborhoods. Air raid wardens were assigned to each neighborhood. In our neighborhood, the wardens were Uncle Andrew Shogan and Mrs. Meredith from down near Larch Street. During practice drills, the street lights were turned off so it would be completely dark. The air raid wardens, wearing white helmets with the civil defense symbol, walked the beat carrying large flashlights and night sticks. They made sure no light was visible from the windows of homes, as everyone had blackout drapes. If the warden saw light coming from your home, they would knock on the door and tell you. If there were any cars out during a drill, they would be stopped and asked to turn off their lights. The curfew whistle would signify the beginning of the drill and once the drill was over, the whistle would sound again to signify "all clear." The drills were done randomly about once a month. No one but the civil defense air raid wardens were permitted to be out during the drills. Mrs. Meredith was a very nice lady and just as silly as Uncle Andrew, so they were a good team. There was a lot of fun and plenty of laughs despite the seriousness of conducting the drills.

The reasons for this concern were the manufacturing of war supplies at the Westinghouse plants and the railroad, which transported troops as well as the manufactured goods. Three full shifts were working the steel mill in Braddock. From the top of the Electric Plan hill, the sky at night, was lighted up orange from the reflection of the blast furnaces.

At that time, all of the companies and schools offered savings plans which supported the war effort. Savings stamps could be purchased from them every week. The stamps were put in a book and once the book was once full, it was redeemed for a government savings bond. You could also sign up to have the amount deducted from your pay at the Westinghouse plants. It was a wonderful way to save money and help the war effort. It encouraged people to form a good habit of saving.

By this time, Uncle John was called back to active duty in the Navy and assigned to a Net-Tender in Newport, Rhode Island. Aunt Florence stayed in Philadelphia. Uncle John stored his new 1941 black, Chevrolet at our house. Aunt Florence didn't drive, so the car would be gently used and garage stored.

This is when I got my driving permit, took my driver's exam and got my license. My father's Willys had a manual shift on the floor and was difficult to drive. My father and Irene taught me how to drive using Uncle John's Chevrolet which was much easier. I passed the exam the first time, but hated driving. I was absolutely terrified of drifting back on the hills. Needless to say, I did not drive much at all.

On April 17, 1942, Irene had her first baby. The first grandchild for my parents, a boy, named John Allan Sapp, would be known as "Jackie." Ironically, tragedy struck on that very same day. Aunt Florence was hospitalized in Philadelphia for routine tests. She was having a test where a scope was put down her throat to investigate trouble she was having with her stomach. While removing it, the doctor ruptured her esophagus and she bled to death on the operating room table. In our joy about Jackie's birth, we immediately had to rush to Philadelphia where we met Uncle John. He was grief-stricken and we stayed with him for the funeral. I just could not believe something so terrible had happened to our dear aunt.

While I was still in high school, I started working part-time at Gordon's Drug Store in the evenings and on weekends. I was working with one of my friends, Antoinette Maroni who lived on Locust Street. While walking home from work one day with Antoinette and Teddy, a car stopped. Walter was driving the car. Eugene Glazer, a classmate of mine, was in the front seat, and Herkie, Walter's younger brother was in the back seat. Walter was very nice looking with dark wavy hair. They asked, "Do you want a ride home?" We said, "Yes" and got in.

A week or so later, I was walking home again. A car pulled up and stopped. This time, it was Walter by himself. He drove me home and asked me for a date. Well, the rest is ancient history. We started dating and had a lot of fun. We went to the drive-in movies. We went roller skating, bike riding and horse-back riding in South Park and played miniature golf. Sometimes Herkie and my cousin, Sylvia would come on a double-date with Walter and me. We loved to go to the Le Barbe on Route 22 in Monroeville near Aunt Dorothy's house. It was a great place with a dance floor, a jukebox and pinball machines. They served up the best pork and ham barbecue sandwiches, French fries, ice cream sundaes and banana splits. We would sit at the Le Barbe for hours, eating ice cream, playing the pinball machines and listening to the jukebox. One of Walter's and Sylvia's favorite songs was "Pistol-Packin' Mama" by Al Dexter. They would play the song over and over again. It truly was a lot of fun.

Le Barbe was owned by Mr. Behler, who was the principal at the high school. Therefore, parents considered it a safe place to hang out. Behind the building, there was a large open-air dance floor where some of the big bands came and performed. In years past, they would hold the high school prom dances there.

*Sylvia and Herkie on a double date with Walter and me
at the Le Barbe in 1942.*

Young and in Love, Walter and me in 1942.

We also went to "Hubba-Hubba" on Crooked Run Road. It was a drive-in restaurant with car hops. They had great hamburgers, French fries, and milkshakes and of course, a big jukebox. I know the boys liked to go there because of the cute car hops. I remember one girl named Rosie who they would all swoon over her.

Walter told me he was waiting to be drafted as he already received one deferment notice. He wanted us to get married and I was fine with that, too. Walter worked on generators at Westinghouse under one of the government contracts. He was also attending night school there at Westinghouse and was trying to get into one of their apprenticeship programs.

Walter was born on June 25, 1921, the very same day as Irene. We always celebrated their birthdays together. In fact, they went to Turtle Creek Union High School and graduated in 1939. While in high school, Walter excelled in math and took vocational classes in machine shop. Many classes in the curriculum at Turtle Creek High School were geared specifically toward careers at the Westinghouse plants. Girls learned office skills and typing. There were opportunities to learn drafting, mechanical drawing, and machine shop. The Westinghouse plant offered wonderful apprenticeship programs and night-school classes to these high school graduates. It was a marvelous way to develop a career without the expense of a college education. Many families in the valley could not afford the luxury of a college education, since they were still recovering from the trying times of the Great Depression. Using his knowledge and developing his technical skills, Walter took advantage of the opportunities with Westinghouse. He passed the entrance exam easily and was hired into one of the apprenticeship programs in May of 1941, where he started working and attending classes at night. It was the beginning of his forty-three year career with Westinghouse.

Walter gave me an engagement ring on the third of October in 1942. It was the same day as Herkie's birthday. We continued to date and decided to elope. We drove to Wellsburg, West Virginia and got married on November 14, 1942. Wellsburg was the place to go and get married without anyone knowing.

We didn't tell my parents that we were married until after the holidays that year as Walter knew he would be drafted in the next group. Many of our friends were also married at the same time as they knew the men were going to be drafted. My parents suspected that we had gotten married and wished us well. They accepted Walter graciously. Walter's parents on the other hand, were very unhappy and not kind. Walter was making payments on and driving a 1939 Oldsmobile. His parents confiscated the car as it was in their name and gave it to one of his brothers. They were not nice people and I kept my distance from them. This was unforgivable as it was very difficult to buy a car during wartime. Even if we could afford one, none were available. We were not able to get a car until our baby, Ronnie, was about a year and a half old, which was in 1945. We borrowed my father's blue Plymouth when we really needed a car; otherwise, we walked or took a bus or streetcar.

My grandmother was unhappy that we were not married in the church. She insisted that we were, so on Valentine's Day, in honor of her wedding anniversary, Walter and I were married in a simple ceremony at Saint Colman's church in Turtle Creek. My cousin, Rita Figulski and neighbor and friend, Tom Gorazd, stood for us. Afterward, my mother had a wedding breakfast at their house for us.

Our "Official" Wedding Day, February 14, 1943.

Once we borrowed my father's Plymouth and went to Turtle Creek to do some shopping. It was very snowy and icy. On the way home, Walter was driving faster than he should have been. As we made the bend onto Locust Street, we started sliding and Walter said "Wweeee!" as we slid right into a telephone pole. I hit the windshield, broke it and ended up with a big knot on my forehead. He didn't think it was funny then.

Walter had a silly, crazy sense of humor. While we were dating, he played a joke on my mother with disappearing ink that he "spilled" on one of her best lace tablecloths. She laughed about it for years. He was a big teaser and very funny. Walter was always horsing around and our children compared him to Dagwood Bumstead.

Like my parents and many others in the family had done before us, we started housekeeping in the two rooms on my grandmother's third floor. It was nice to be there with my grandmother, having her right downstairs. Aunt Betty, Uncle Joe, and their two young daughters, Connie and Margie lived there, too. It was a busy, active house as it always was.

We started buying furniture and moved in. There was no electric refrigerator but we used an old ice box. Sometimes, I would keep food in grandmother's refrigerator downstairs. In the winter, there was a small window box, much like the one my parents had. New appliances were absolutely unheard of and not available because of wartime production. Nearly a year after we were married, we found a used refrigerator. My father's friend, Henry Carfagna owned a furniture store in Turtle Creek. He told my father he had a used Westinghouse refrigerator that we could buy. It sure beat the ice box and having to empty that pan of water every day. Walter's salary was only $28.54 a week as an apprentice at Westinghouse while he was going school, so we could not afford to buy much.

We managed to buy a couple of chairs, a radio-phonograph, a kitchen table with chairs and a bedroom set. I really wanted Virginia-House Maple for our bedroom, as I liked the color and finish of the wood. The only furniture that Mr. Carfagna had in that finish was a boy's bedroom set with a full sized bed. It had been carved with an airplane motif and had a huge propeller carved into the wood on the foot board of the bed. We decided to buy it anyway, as later when we had children, we could use it. The finish was beautiful, as was the carving. It was quite nice.

Little Connie was only about 5 years old and her sister, Margie was about 3 years old when they liked to come upstairs to visit with us. Silly Walter told them one day, "When Minnie and I hop into the bed at night, when you are fast asleep, that propeller starts spinning and we fly all around." Apparently, when we were out, the girls used to sneak up to our bedroom and just stare at the bed in amazement. Connie told us of that many years later.

In August of 1943, Walter and Jack were drafted and shipped out on the same train going from McKeesport to Camp Meade. By this time, the male cousins had either been drafted or enlisted in some branch of the military. Some of them were in the Army as Walter and Jack had been others in the Navy, Marines, or Air Force. Most of them left on troop trains from the East

Pittsburgh station on the backside of the Westinghouse plant. Entry to the train platform was actually inside the Westinghouse plant.

High School Graduation, 1943.

If you had a son or daughter in the service at the time, you were given a small flag for each of them to be displayed proudly in your front window. Many of the homes on Electric Plan had flags in their windows. Unfortunately, some of them displayed gold stars on those flags which indicated a life had been lost while serving the country during the war. Each day, we would follow the news on the radio and in the newspaper and hope the war would soon be over.

Once, someone said the Sears and Roebucks department store in East Liberty was getting a shipment of nylon stockings. Stockings simply were not available as they were not being made. Instead, the nylon was being used for parachutes for the war. Irene and I were so anxious to get some so we convinced my father to drive us there. We waited in line for hours and hours and finally ended up getting our stockings. Three pairs per person was the limit. During these times, leg makeup was available that gave your legs a pale, soft appearance as if you were wearing stockings.

From Camp Meade, Walter was sent to Camp Crowder near Springfield, Missouri. Jack was dispatched into a position in the motor pool and was first sent to Louisiana, then Germany. After Walter was at Camp Crowder for a few weeks, he got very sick and passed out. He was sent to O'Reilly Hospital in Springfield, Missouri. After some tests were done, they discovered he had a tumor on his pituitary gland. It would require surgical removal and he stayed there during his recovery. It was decided that Walter would be discharged as he would only be able to do limited duty activities. He was officially discharged and arrived home on May 22, 1944. On the very next day, May 23, I gave birth to our first child, Ronald Walter Lawrence.

On April 15, 1945, our cousin, Maria, then imprisoned in Bergen-Belsen, was released. The British liberated the camp and the torture of the Nazis was over. They were sent to a displacement camp in Germany, where they could receive medical attention, try to contact family members and be sent to other countries to start new lives. Maria immediately started to teach in a school there for the people that were in the camps. This is where she eventually met and married her husband, Kazu. She had no desire to return to Poland where her family was still living as she was still fearful. She was given the choice of going to live in Canada or the United States. My father and other members of his family started the paperwork for her sponsorship to come to the United States. It was a miracle she survived the camps.

Walter returned to his job at the Westinghouse plant and his apprenticeship studies. We tried to save our money so we could go out on our own. I put Ronnie in his stroller and walked down to my parents' house to do the laundry. I also took him with me down the hill into Turtle Creek to do shopping. Mrs. Palmer opened a small store on Locust Street, by that time.

On Saturdays, we usually went with my parents to do other shopping. Walter finally saved enough money to buy a used car at Limegrover's Oldsmobile in Turtle Creek. It was a gray 1939 model like he used to have, but it had been in a wreck. There was some slight damage to the grill in the front and they sold it "as is," so we got it for a good price.

It was now 1945 and it was time for us to move out on our own. We got a place in the Electric Heights Housing Project at 97-A Harper Drive. Many of the workers who had come to live there during the war, stayed on. Many of them found other jobs, but some continued to work in the Westinghouse plants. It was a cute, three-room place with a small yard for Ronnie. It had a utility room, so I was able to get my own washing machine.

*Ronnie, Walter, and me in front of our 1939 Oldsmobile
on Electric Plan in 1945.*

Our neighbors were all very nice. Next door to us lived Bill and Dorothy Bard and their two girls, Darla and Darleen. Ronnie loved playing in the yard and I would take him for walks, sometimes down on the Indian path to visit my parents and go to Palmers store. When he was a little older, he would ride his tricycle around on the sidewalks.

I made all of my window coverings and sewed cute red and white checked curtains for the kitchen. It was small but it was ours. Ronnie made friends with Frankie Figolia, whose family lived in the next row over from us. They would play together often. From the time Ronnie was born, he got my undivided attention. There was no television then and all day long we would listen to music and play as I did my housework and cooked meals. In the evenings, as we would read stories, I would point to the words. By the time Ronnie started school, he was very smart.

Once, when Ronnie was very small and we first moved to Harper Drive, Walter had gone to work and Ronnie and I were at home alone. The sky became very, very dark. Something just didn't seem to be right. Suddenly, a severe electrical storm developed. I was absolutely petrified. The electricity went out and the thunder boomed and actually rattled the windows. Lightening danced in the skies around our place and the rain came down in torrents. I took a blanket and draped it over the kitchen table. I grabbed Ronnie and we crawled under the table. There was no basement and I thought we'd be safer there until the storm was over. All of a sudden there was a knock at the door. Thank goodness, it was my father. He came in the car to check on us and took us home with him where we stayed until the storm passed. I've always hated storms as did my mother. Every time there was a storm, Irene used to tease me about it. She would say, "Get under the kitchen table, Minnie!"

One cold afternoon, I had just put Ronnie down for a nap and was going to take a rest myself. I thought I heard a faint tapping noise. In a few minutes, I thought I heard it again. I couldn't figure out where it was coming from. I looked outside to discover three year old Jackie, standing and knocking on my door. He got away from Irene and my mother and they couldn't find him anywhere. He walked to our house through the woods on the Indian path. It was a cold afternoon and he was wearing a sweater, his underpants, no shoes and boxing gloves!

One day, Irene and I decided to surprise my mother and make Polish filled doughnuts, called paczkis. Irene was in charge of the project and I was to be her assistant. We got all of the ingredients organized and she scalded the milk to dissolve the yeast. Apparently, Irene was in a hurry and she didn't cool the milk enough before she added the yeast. We mixed everything together and waited for the dough to rise. We waited and waited and waited, but it didn't seem the dough was rising. We decided to test one of the donuts in the hot grease, but it sank to the bottom, stayed there and didn't float on top as they are supposed to. Irene thought instead of frying them, we could bake them. That's exactly what we did and they turned out like hand grenades. They were hard as a rock! We tossed the mess into the garbage and decided to leave the paczkis making up to my mother. Years later, we made them together and laughed and laughed about our first try. Irene and I could be just like Lucy and Ethel.

Irene with Jackie, and me with Ronnie, swimming
at Rainbow Gardens in 1946.

When Ronnie was about two years old, one afternoon I decided we would walk down to visit my parents. Irene and her young son, Jackie were also at my mother's and I thought it would be nice if the boys could play together. The boys were playing and having a lot of fun but it was starting to get late and I wanted to walk back home as I had things to do. I started to dress Ronnie with his coat and noticed he was starting to get little red spots on his face and arms. He had the measles. It was cold outside and if I took Ronnie out, the measles could have gotten much worse. Of course, Jackie got them a few hours later. The boys were thrilled. It turned into a week-long stay at grandma's house and when they weren't sleeping, they were playing together. Irene and I were there for the duration too. The only casualty during the measle-pajama party was Ronnie's goldfish. Walter forgot all about him.

Work at the Westinghouse plant had its ups and downs. Toward the end of the war, there were slowdowns and during one period when Walter wasn't working, I got a job. It was a temporary position at Redlick's Furniture Factory in the Homewood section of Pittsburgh. Irene was also working second shift there, so we went to work together. Sometimes, Irene would drive when Jack didn't need the car. Other times, we would take the streetcar and walk. I was a riveter on the assembly line, making tables and chairs. They were the chrome and metal ones which were popular then. It was a fun job and I liked it, but it only lasted a few months. It was my turn at being "Maryann, the Riveter" like "Rosie, the Riveter."

By this time, most of the cousins were back from active duty. We were so very fortunate that our family did not lose anyone during the war. It was a miracle. Many were already married and others were getting married and starting young families just like the rest of us. Family gatherings were large and a lot of fun. This was the beginning of a new generation that would play together and remain as close as the generation before. It was good to see that happening and I know that it warmed the heart of my grandmother. The bond in our family was so strong and watching that continue was incredible.

We loaded up the Oldsmobile and took a vacation trip to Atlantic City, New Jersey, during the summer. We took Irene and Jackie with us. We always stopped in Philadelphia to visit with Aunt Mayme and Uncle Joe O'Brien. We found a place to stay in Pleasantville, New Jersey, outside of Atlantic City, as it was only a short drive to the beach and it was less expensive. We always went to a bakery there and got huge, fresh cinnamon buns and pecan rolls to have for breakfast at the motel. We went swimming at the beach in the afternoons. We always took our cooler and packed sandwiches for lunch. Ronnie and Jackie loved playing in the sand and wading in the surf. We took them to see "Lucy, the Elephant" at Margate. We had dinner at a great diner called Giberson's in Pleasantville and then strolled on the boardwalk in the evening. We made this trip several times throughout the years. The beach was always so beautiful and it was fun to play in the water with the children. It was the same trip that our parents had taken with us as children, when times were good and there was money to spend. There are many happy memories of times we spent on the Jersey shore.

On December 2, 1947, Irene had her second child, Joseph Virgil Sapp, Joseph and I share the same birthday. We were slowly outgrowing the small place on Harper Drive and asked at the office if we could move into a larger unit. We moved into a two story, two bedroom unit at 91-B Harper

Drive. Many of the cousins and other relatives moved into Electric Heights Housing, after starting housekeeping at my grandmother's home and stayed there.

My friend, Teddy, married one of Walter's close friends, Albert (Cab) Winners. They started by living in the Electric Heights Housing Project until they saved money to buy a house. The rent was affordable. There were rules to obey and the best part was that then everyone there knew each other and got along well. It was like one big, happy family. The housing units were small but at the entrance, there was a large rental office, where they had a huge kitchen that could be used for large parties and events. Beyond that was Hilltop Hall which was a very large brick building like a gymnasium that was used for community events. There were also some playground areas throughout the grounds with swings, slides and other equipment and basketball courts. The entire area was still surrounded by woods which also gave the children other places to play. It was an ideal place to raise a family.

We moved into 91-B Harper Drive and enjoyed more nice neighbors and additional space. On one side of us, lived the Thomas family and they had eight children. On the other side, was a young couple, Adam and Kay Santavicca and their young boys. Nearly every Friday, Mrs. Thomas handed us a loaf of home-baked bread. As Walter walked up the sidewalk from work one day, the young Thomas girls asked him what he was going to have for dinner. He replied, "Well, soup-sandwiches, of course!" It sent them into hysterics of silly laughter and they remember that to this day. He loved to have fun teasing the kids.

On January 12, 1949, I gave birth to Bonita Louise Lawrence. Everyone was absolutely thrilled as she was the first girl and first and only granddaughter that my parents had. When my grandmother found out that I was expecting, she asked me to name the baby "Bonnie," after the little girl in her favorite movie, "Gone with the Wind." That's exactly what we named her. She was my father's little "Princess." The boys called her "sissy" which was short for sister.

It was that fall when Ronnie began to attend a Kindergarten at Hilltop Hall gymnasium. Theora Judge was the teacher and everyone knew her as she also lived on Harper Drive. She was very nice and had a little boy of her own. Ronnie went to the morning session with his friends, our neighbors, Gloria Thomas and Harriet Kull. Ronnie's first grade teacher was Mrs. Hughes. The Hughes family lived on James Street in a small white clapboard house with green trim, next to the Overlook Tavern. Mrs. Hughes was a nice, old-fashioned type of person. For Christmas in her class, the students made a cookie recipe book for their mothers. They made the cover of the book from black construction paper and glued a cut-out picture of Santa Claus on the front. They wove red ribbon around the edge to make a border and to teach them how to weave ribbon through holes. Mrs. Hughes made copies of eight cookie recipes, allowing a page for each one. It was clipped together with a brass acorn clip. I made the delicious sugar cookie recipe for Christmas every year for my children. I still have the recipe book Ronnie gave me for Christmas that year and it is one of my treasures. It was a really nice gift to receive from a first grader.

On Columbus Day, October 14, 1949, our cousin, Maria and her husband, Kazu got off of the train in Braddock. At last, they were free and their struggles were over and they were now in America to start a new life. On October 15, everyone in my father's family welcomed them with a huge party held at the home of Cecelia and Frank Zygmunt. It was truly an event to mark the end of the "War Years" and to enable us to get on with life and our families.

Walter, Ronnie, baby Bonnie, and me on Easter 1949.

My Family
and Our Life in the 1950s

Our lives continued to be much the same as we settled into living in a new decade. The 1950s brought many changes for all of us. These were some of the happiest years for all of us.

Little Bonnie was growing up nicely. She started walking early but was late to start talking. She was always very quiet, anyway. In fact, she would sit and play for hours with Marion Shogan's little girl, Jeanne Lewandowski. Neither one would ever say a word. Kay Santavicca and I would take turns making eggs for breakfast as Bonnie preferred only the whites and her son, Domenick preferred only the yolks. We laughed about that for years.

In 1950, we experienced the biggest snowfall of my lifetime. It started in the morning on Thanksgiving Day. Big flakes started falling and the sky was very dark as we looked out of the window on Harper Drive. We thought it was going to be a bad one. I made pies for Thanksgiving at my parents' house and dinner was going to be at one o'clock in the afternoon. We drove with the children to their house and by the time we finished our meal, the roads were really getting bad. We didn't linger and got back into the car for the drive home. We hardly made it back home as the snow was really coming down and the roads were very treacherous. By that evening, the temperature dropped to five degrees and stayed there for the next few days. The wind picked up and the snow started blowing. By Friday morning, we had about eight inches of snow. The wind continued to blow and howl. The storm continued through Saturday. At one point, we looked outside and could not see beyond the sidewalk. On Sunday, we awoke to about two feet of snow. There was a warning on the radio to stay indoors as at least another foot of snow was expected before the storm was over. By Monday morning, snow had reached the top of the windowsills. In all, we officially had a thirty six inch snowfall. Everything was closed for about three days and there were no deliveries. When Ronnie went outside in his snowsuit, we couldn't even see him. It took a long time for plows to clear the streets. Walter bundled up and walked to the Clover Farm Market and the shelves were nearly bare. He continued on to Philbert's Market on James Street and then to Aunt Jean's store on Maple Avenue, just to get bread and milk. It is now known as "The Big Snow of 1950" and it was surely a snowfall that we'll never forget.

In the years after the war, there were many changes, even on Electric Plan. Houses were starting to be built on the newer section of Locust Street. They were brick, story and one half-style houses, built by Mr. Canobio. They were also building houses on the streets below Locust Street. Mr. Madden was building houses on Mercer Street, James Street, and George Street. They were very cute little houses and they had nice yards.

Walter and I saved up enough money and purchased a house at 658 Mercer Street. It was built in 1949 by Mr. Madden and originally sold to a couple by the name of Hoffman. They weren't there for very long until their marriage ended in divorce. So the house was put up for sale. We purchased it for $10,500 and moved in January, 1951. It was so wonderful to experience the pride of home ownership and to have so much more room. The house was a nice brick story and one half-style, with an integral garage, full basement, and a very nice large lot. It had beautiful Venetian plaster walls, arched doorways and gorgeous hardwood floors. The front yard was a little hilly, but the backyard was nice for the kids to play in. Behind the back fence was an easement with a small path, some woods and apple trees.

Ronnie and the "Big Snow of 1950."

Bonnie and Ronnie on Harper Drive in 1951.

The second floor was not finished, but had enough space for two bedrooms. Walter and my father finished them and eventually we had a dormer put out in the back that added a bathroom and increased the bedroom space dramatically. There was a small attic storage space in the front.

When we bought the house, my grandmother bought us a rose bush as our housewarming gift. It was so beautiful when it bloomed. We took special care of it as it always reminded us of her. When we sold the home thirty four years later, the rose bush was transplanted into Bonnie's yard. From there, it was moved once, when they changed houses and is now at her former home in Harrison City. I often wish I had a planting from it now as a remembrance to my grandmother and the years I enjoyed the rose bush and its beautiful flowers.

We were busy with our new home and improving it to make it our own. Ronnie and Bonnie really liked it there and had a nice yard to play in. When the weather was cold or rainy, they played in the large basement. They would draw on their chalkboard or show their View master projector on the walls. They had plenty of toys to keep them entertained. They used their imaginations and were never bored. At one point, my father bought Bonnie, a Dale Evans play outfit, complete with cap guns and holster. It had a fringed cowgirl skirt and vest, boots, and a hat. He also bought her a Roy Rogers canvas tent that we would set up in the back yard. They would play for hours. We had a sliding board, swing set, and a swimming pool. They had so much fun playing outdoors. I often fixed Ronnie and Bonnie a lunch which they would eat in the tent and pretend. Cowboys and westerns were quite popular with both children and adults.

Ronnie and Bonnie would go on adventures walking down the path behind our house to Ella Kingston's store which was at the end of Locust Street. They would buy penny candy and popsicles. They would walk there and back on the path through the woods behind the house. They had their share of bumps, cuts, and skinned knees. Bonnie once tried putting her knee into a magazine slot on the side of my coffee table in the living room. We caught her just in time, before she slipped her head in between the bars of the decorative wrought iron stair railing. They were just normal children, investigating and having fun.

We shared a special friendship for many years with our next door neighbors, Lloyd and Louise Brown. Lloyd, whose nickname was "Brownie," was a Turtle Creek native from Mobile Avenue. Louise was originally from a little town called Dunbar near Mt. Pleasant. They bought their house right after it had been built. They had no children and became very close to our family. They were very nice people and a lot of fun. Louise was a small, petite woman who wore her hair pulled up. I can still hear her calling in a sing-song little voice from her open kitchen window "Maarryaannnn! Whatcha doin?" She'd come bouncing outside with a Viceroy cigarette in her lips and a bottle of Coca cola. She would sit on the concrete steps by her trellis, near our wall and we could chat for hours. We had many enjoyable times together.

Walter went to work one day and I wanted to take the kids to visit Irene and the boys. Jack, Irene and her boys were living with Jack's parents on the top of Pitcairn hill. The only way to get there was to drive. We had a green, 1950 Pontiac Catalina that Walter bought from Bob Constantine, a Pontiac dealer on Baum Boulevard. It was a beautiful car but I had not driven it. It had a manual transmission with the shift on the column and I had to go to the top of Pitcairn hill and I was so afraid of drifting backwards. I was bound and determined to drive us to see my sister and that's just what I did. Once I got the car into second gear, that's where I left it the entire way. Everyone laughed and said I could have ruined the transmission driving it for miles in second gear. We made it there and we made it back home so I did what I was determined to do.

Once under the G.I. bill, Walter went to meat cutting school. He never did any related work but he certainly could carve the Thanksgiving turkey. During another strike at the Westinghouse plant, Walter and his friend, Ray Berta got jobs at a machine company on Euclid Avenue in Cleveland. They rented a room and stayed there during the week and drove home on weekends. They worked there for three months during the duration of the strike.

One time, during a strike at the Westinghouse plant, I decided to go to business school. I went to the Florence Utt Business School in downtown Pittsburgh. The school was later known as the Bradford Business School. I really enjoyed it and completed my course of study. After business school, I worked for a short time in the office at a department store, called The Famous, in Braddock. Irene worked there at the time. They needed some extra help, so I was hired. I was one of the telephone operators and also helped with other general office duties. They had a pneumatic tube system and the clerk would send a sales slip with the customer's money to you. I would make the correct change and send it back in the tube to the clerk to give to the customer. I counted the change in my head without the use of a calculator or computer. Amazing!

One day, when I was going downtown to business school, I needed my mother to watch the kids. I took them over to my parents' house. My mother was watching Irene's boys and thought it would be great for the kids to play together. Sometimes, it was good, sometimes it was not. Irene's youngest boy, Joey was usually the instigator. Joey and Bonnie were playing in my parents' basement. In the back basement, where my mother kept canned goods, they had a few things stored, among which was her old Maytag wringer washing machine. Joey was a couple years older than Bonnie and could easily tell her what to do and she would obey. He talked her into playing "space-ship" inside of the old washing machine. He told her to climb inside and she did. Joey promptly closed the lid and put a box on top of it. He turned out the light and shut the door and proceeded to go outside to play with the other children. Bonnie started to panic, screaming and crying but no one could hear her. After a while my mother started to wonder where Bonnie was. She couldn't find her anywhere. My mother was just frantic. She asked Joey and he told her he didn't know where she was. Eventually, they heard her screams from the back basement and my mother rescued her. Bonnie was frightened and never forgave Joey for what he did to her. My mother certainly didn't "spare the rod" that day and gave Joey a lesson that hopefully, he never forgot.

Recreation was always a lot of fun for us. We liked to go fishing and always took a picnic lunch to make a whole day of it. We went to Pymatuning Reservoir, Lake Erie, Fisherman's Paradise near Altoona, Keystone, and Mountain Valley. One time, we took Irene, Jack and their boys to Lake Erie to go fishing. We promised my father some freshly caught fish, ready to fry. We spent hours fishing with not a single bite. We decided to leave and on the way home, the car got stuck in a ditch and we had to get someone to pull us out. We ended up buying fresh fish on the way home and put them in a container with ice. That was an expensive fishing trip. We laughed about it for years, but we still took fish home to my father.

Bonnie, Ronnie, and me in Philadelphia in 1952.

On a trip to Fisherman's Paradise, the weather turned cold, and we caught no fish. On the way home, Bonnie kept telling us that she smelled keilbasy and she was absolutely insistent. Every few miles, she kept saying "I smell keilbasy.", "I smell kielbasy." Just outside of Tyrone, Pennsylvania, we spotted a smoke house off in the distance and sure enough, they were making keilbasy. We stopped there and bought some of the best home-made keilbasy that Bonnie could smell miles away.

One year, Jack and Irene promised to take Ronnie fishing for his birthday. They drove up to Pymatuning Reservoir and went fishing. On the way home, Jack was speeding. They were pulled over by the police outside of Portersville on Route 79. When the policeman approached the car, Ronnie immediately started to cry hysterically. He thought they were all going to go to jail. He said to the officer, "Mr. Policeman, it's my birthday. Don't take us to jail!" The policeman laughed, warned Jack about speeding, wished Ronnie a "Happy Birthday", and sent them on their way without a ticket.

We loaded up the car one day and took Marion (Shogan) and Freddy Lewandowski and the kids to Idlewild Park for a picnic. We took a big picnic basket full of sandwiches and goodies. We claimed a table in one of the picnic areas and left the basket there to save our spot. We ran off with the kids to enjoy amusement rides and play miniature golf. Everyone was getting hungry. It was around lunch time, so we headed back to the table to set up our picnic and eat. Marion and I opened up the picnic basket and discovered someone swapped the sandwiches. They took the good ones we brought from home and left ones that weren't as good in their place. We decided to skip the sandwiches and buy funnel cakes and ice cream instead. It was a tasty lunch that we had that day.

Often, we would take Irene and her boys with us when Jack was working and they would take us with them, too. We shared a lot of laughs and many adventures together. Jack was as crazy as Walter, so together, they were quite a combination. One day my kids asked Jack about the lack of hair on his head as he was balding. His reply to them was, "Trees don't grow on a busy street!"

A couple years after we bought our house, Irene and Jack bought a house in Fairhaven Heights, off of Foster Road in East McKeesport. It was a nice brick ranch style house with a large basement. Bonnie begged us to go to "Renie's house" for a pajama party, so one night, she did just that. It lasted until about two o'clock in the morning. They had to drive her home as Bonnie was crying because she was homesick.

Summertime always saw many outings. We went on picnics, played miniature golf or went to the driving range to hit golf balls. Walter's brother, Herkie and his cousin owned "Angle Tangle", which was a miniature golf course in Monroeville where the Miracle Mile Plaza is now. We often went to Kennywood Park to ride the amusement rides. We would go there for the school picnics held at the end of each school year. One year, it was so cold; I remember I dressed Bonnie in her winter coat. We also went to Kennywood Park for Westinghouse Family Day, and sometimes for Polish Day or Italian Day. The park honored special days for every nationality in Pittsburgh, and held many company picnics. We also went to the county fair which was always held by South Park. We would go swimming at Burke's Glen or to the pool at Rainbow Gardens. There were always many things to do.

My grandmother and mother, sharing lunch together in 1952.

Sometimes, we would go with my parents to the auctions which were usually held in the Auction Barn on Route 30. We would have supper first at a diner called The Circle, then go over to the auction. The Circle was a typical diner with the classic diner atmosphere with the best food one could ever imagine. The menu included gigantic fish sandwiches, and beef, ham and pork barbecues. Specialties they were known for. It was always so crowded on Friday and Saturday nights. They had a big old jukebox that was always playing and pinball machines off to the side just like the LeBarbe. The waitresses could hardly get through the crowd, balancing their plates of food, as kids would be dancing to the music in the aisles. It was a lively place and we always enjoyed going there. After we would eat supper, we would all go over to the auction. The auction was pure entertainment and you would never know what you might come home with. The auctioneers were two rotund, brothers that always wore overhauls and they had the craziest sense of humor. My father and Walter would always run into someone there that they knew. It really was entertainment and fun.

The kids always enjoyed the drive-in movies. There were many drive-in theatres and we usually went to Greater Pittsburgh Drive-in at the top of the hill by the Greater Valley shopping center. We wondered just how much of the movie the kids really saw or how many snacks they ate before they fell asleep.

In the summer months, usually on Friday nights, a man would come to the playground at the Electric Plan School and show movies outdoors with his projector. He showed cartoons and Disney movies. Louise Brown and I took a blanket and some snacks and would walk over with the kids. We stopped and visited with my parents first along the way and then walked down and watched the movie. Going home, the kids would always be thirsty so we asked Mrs. Laurito for a drink of water from her pump. Sometimes, Louise and I would treat them to milkshakes at Janet's Dairy store on Maple Avenue. Jenny Nellis, the owner made the best home-made ham salad.

There were many big snowfalls in those days, but none ever compared to the one in 1950. We always helped Walter clear the driveway as there was no other way to get the car in or out of the garage. Neighbors helped neighbors in those days, so once we got ours cleared, we would go next door and help Louise and Brownie clear their driveway. Walter and I would take the kids sled riding and they would have a lot of fun. One year, Bonnie got a new style fiberglass saucer sled and could even use it in the backyard. We decorated the house for Christmas with colorful lights wound around the front porch railings. My father bought us some colorful plastic holiday lanterns that lit up that we hung on each pillar of the front porch. I always had a big wreath on the front door. Brownie put out a Santa, sleigh and reindeer in his front yard for the kids to enjoy. Every Christmas Eve, after we returned home from my parents' house, we went over to the Brown's. It was a tradition. The tree in their living room was impeccably trimmed with beautiful glass ornaments. Christmas music would be playing softly on the Hi-Fi. The clear plastic covers were removed from the brocade French provincial furniture and Louise would serve fresh baked Christmas cookies and delicious home-made eggnog. We would exchange gifts and visit. Then the kids were taken home and put to bed, anticipating Santa. We enjoyed live Christmas trees and the kids had their electric train on a platform under the tree. It was never as elaborate as the one we would continue to enjoy at the home of my parents. My father saw to it that each of his grandchildren had their own train. That was very important to him. My father continued with his Christmas displays for the children until he became ill.

My parents in 1953.

Once Bonnie was in school for the whole day, I decided to go to work. Like everyone else, I went to Westinghouse. I was the "dessert lady" in the cafeteria. I would work from eleven o'clock in the morning until two o'clock in the afternoon. I really worked quickly to keep up with the lunch crowd. I sliced pies and cakes as fast as I could. Ice cream was served and I cleaned up afterwards. It was like working a ten hour day in three hours. I worked there for about a year and then decided the job wasn't for me. I worked with Dolores Jones. Her husband was my father's friend. She had a little girl, Beverly. The Jones moved near us on George Street. Bonnie and Beverly became the best of playmates.

The "little princess" of ours was something else. Bonnie's favorite color was purple and she loved it in any shade. Everything she wanted had to be purple. Shades of orchid or lavender would do just fine. My sister, Irene had a wool coat in a pretty shade of orchid. Bonnie admired her coat every time Irene wore it. She would say, "Renie, I love your purple coat." It was time for Bonnie to get a new coat and of course, she wanted "a purple one, just like Renie's." We searched everywhere, high and low with no luck at all and could not find a purple coat anywhere. One day, Irene showed up with a beautiful, orchid wool coat and matching hat for Bonnie. She took her coat apart, got a pattern for a child's coat and matching hat, and made it for Bonnie. It was so beautiful and fit Bonnie so perfectly. Bonnie loved it so much that she wore it until it was a size too small for her. Irene really surprised all of us, but it was a special surprise for Bonnie. The purple stage continued and we had to paint her bedroom a soft shade of orchid. We bought light orchid bedspreads for her twin poster beds and orchid curtains. She had to have orchid and purple dresses and I even made the same in dotted Swiss for her dolls.

I was so hungry for stuffed green peppers that I decided to make some and invited Jack, Irene and their boys for dinner. The peppers turned out beautifully and I made mashed potatoes to accompany them. I got some new dark green plastic bowls for serving and decided to use them for the peppers, mashed potatoes, and the sauce. I had the table all set and put the new bowls full of my delicious dinner on the table. As we sat down to eat, the children started yelling and then laughing. Right before our very eyes, the new plastic bowls started to melt and our delicious dinner was starting to pour all over my table. The edges of the bowl with the hot mashed potatoes, was actually scalloped by the heat. I guess those new plastic bowls were not heat resistant. It was a mess to clean up and my delicious dinner went right into the trash. We all piled into the car and went out to the L&B in East McKeesport for dinner. We still had a good time. No more plastic dishes for me!

Every morning, the kids would watch Captain Kangaroo on television to start their day. As soon as the show was over, the television went off until American Bandstand came on at three o'clock. I would open the top of the Magnavox Hi-Fi and play stacks of records all day long. My children grew up with music the same way I did. There was always a strong love for music in our family and our home was filled with it every day. I played Walter's 78's, our albums, and then the kids 45's. Bonnie loved "The Crawdad Song" by Burl Ives and Walter would play it for her over and over again. I'd sing along to Rosemary Clooney's "This Ole House" to Kenny when he was a baby and he remembers that to this day. Walter would drop his voice to a deep baritone and teasingly sing along with Fats Domino "in the Valley of Tears." He always liked that song. We bought records regularly, many of which we still have today. We often went to see live shows downtown at the Warner and Stanley theatres, like Nat King Cole, Rosemary Clooney, the McGuire Sisters, and the Mills Brothers.

Ronnie and Bonnie in front of our home at 658 Mercer Street in 1954.

Walter, Ronnie, Bonnie, and me on the back patio in 1954.

We even enjoyed early rock and roll with the kids, like Connie Francis, and the Everly Brothers, and we even liked some of Elvis' music. Pat Boone, Gale Storm, Kay Starr, Ernie Ford, Patsy Cline, the Platters and the Drifters, and many more graced our turntable every day. One of our favorite songs from that time was the "Tennessee Waltz" by Patti Page and that 78 record is worn thin.

Walter decided to go back to school in 1955. He was always fascinated with television in its early days and truly wanted to take his career in a different direction. We got our first television in 1950, when we lived on Harper Drive. It was a Westinghouse model with a twelve inch round screen. Programming was very limited in those days and it was only in black and white. The picture would be very snowy sometimes, with poor reception. I remember watching Al Morgan play the piano and Kay Neuman doing a cooking show, not to mention Ed Sullivan, Milton Berle and the Goldbergs. Allegheny Technical Institute was offering a two year program in television repair and camera operations. Walter immediately enrolled and he absolutely loved it. He completed the two year course and graduated in July of 1957. He was offered a position as a camera man at a network television station in Baltimore, Maryland. My parents would hear nothing of the like. They would not have us moving away from them and that was that. After all, Westinghouse provided a fine living for all of our family and we should never forget it. Walter always regretted not taking the job. A man who graduated with him accepted that position, after Walter turned it down, and eventually retired from that same television station many years later. Another man who went to school with Walter was one of the founders of WQED in Pittsburgh. It was a public television station that was just starting and he approached Walter about working with him, but allegiance to Westinghouse was already decided.

Once we moved into our house, we wanted to get a dog for the kids. Ronnie wanted one desperately. The Browns had a black chow mix, named Topsy and she was very sweet. She was always kissing the kids through the back fence. Irene's boys had Smokey, a water spaniel mix and my father's pal. Grandma Sapp, Jack's mother gave Ronnie money to go to the pound and get a dog. Walter took Ronnie and they brought home a beautiful golden colored cocker spaniel named Sandy. We put Sandy outside on the back patio and Ronnie went out to pet the dog and Sandy promptly snapped at him. Sandy was taken back to the pound. Sandy was owned by two spinster school teachers who were moving away. I guess the dog was not used to children. Ronnie was heartbroken. In July of 1957, Cookie, the butcher at the A&P grocery store, told Uncle Joe Evancho that his dog had puppies and asked if he knew anyone that would want one. Connie Evancho brought "Rusty" to us in a tin pie pan. He was only about six weeks old and just adorable. He had a beautiful rust color coat, was such a cute puppy and grew into a wonderful dog and a member of our family. He was a medium sized mixed breed with a sweet disposition. As soon as he could slip out of the back door, he would roam Electric Plan. He always returned home. It was a true miracle that he never was hit by a car on James Street, the way many other dogs in the neighborhood met their early demise. I'm so thankful that was something we never had to face with him as he was like another child to us.

We bought a new 1957 Chevy Belair station wagon and I started driving more. It had an automatic transmission and power steering! It was a pretty car and it was actually a pleasure to drive. For once in my life, I didn't mind driving. It was a rust and white two-tone with stylish fins and the perfect size. I would drive the children to school and go shopping. It was great.

That summer, we decided to take the kids on a couple of trips. We knew another baby was on the way, so we wanted to make summer vacation special. We took them to sight-see in New York City. We enjoyed the Statue of Liberty, Radio City Music Hall, and other sights there. We took them to eat at the "automat" one day. The kids enjoyed seeing the food in the little windows, like a display case. When you put in the correct amount of coins, the window would open and you would take the food that you wanted. We also went to Atlantic City to the beach at Ventnor, as we usually did and stopped to visit all of the historic places in Philadelphia. The kids enjoyed seeing Independence Hall, the Liberty Bell, and the Betsy Ross house. Of course, we stopped to see Aunt Mayme and Uncle Joe O'Brien as we always did when we would go to the shore. The kids really enjoyed them and they enjoyed the kids.

It was sunny and warm, just like a spring day, when Kenny was born on February 23 in 1958. He was a chubby baby and I swear he didn't sleep for his entire first year. We finally put a radio on in the bedroom and that helped Kenny sleep.

Bonnie was in the fourth grade then, and her teacher was Mrs. Jane Lawrence, who was formerly Miss Jane Wilson, a teacher that I had many years before. She knitted a beautiful yellow sweater for Kenny. Mrs. Lawrence was Kenny's fourth grade teacher, the year she retired. I sent her a beautiful tapestry handbag as a retirement gift. She was a nice person and a good teacher, but no relation to the Lawrence family. I never forgot her kindness.

I always made time to participate in activities and projects at the school with the children and the teachers. I knew all of the teachers and they knew me. I was homeroom mother for all three of my children every year from first to sixth grade. It was usually me and Mrs. Muir for Ronnie's class, and it was me and Mildred Keister for Bonnie's class, and several mothers helped me with Kenny's class. The teachers knew they could count on us to help them with parties and special events and they knew who baked the best cookies! The second grade teacher, Myrtle Patterson, always made butter with her class as a project using an old fashioned churn. Each child took a turn churning it and when it was done, she served it on crackers. In the third grade, Theora Judge was the teacher, so I knew her from Ronnie's kindergarten. For Thanksgiving, she made soup with her class. Each child took a bowl, a spoon and a vegetable. I took our electric Westinghouse roaster and the soup was served to the class to teach them about preparing a meal together for Thanksgiving. Mrs. Judge's "soup day" as it was called, was a tradition at the Electric Plan School and she did it until she retired. It was great fun and the kids enjoyed it. There were parties in the classroom for each holiday and then, as homeroom mother, you went along to help the teacher on field trips. There were many trips to dairy farms, the Pittsburgh Zoo, the Heinz factory where everyone got a pickle pin, and many rides on the Gateway Clipper. Once the junior high dances started, I was chosen to be a regular chaperone. It was a lot of fun and the children were very well behaved. There were never issues with their behavior and it was a joy to participate in these activities and be a part of their growing up.

I always drove the kids to school in the morning and picked them up at lunch at Electric Plan School. Once Ronnie was in high school, I still usually drove them. Sometimes they would walk if I didn't have the car. Many days, while driving from the school, I'd see Florence End. She was the music teacher and would be walking to her house on James Street. I'd always give her a ride and she would say, "Thanks, Maryann!" I was just getting ready to take the kids to school one morning and there was a knock on our front door.

Kenny in early 1959.

There stood Miss Kinsey, the reading teacher, and her sister, Mrs. Speelman, who taught first grade, shivering in the cold. Their car broke down on James Street. They knew I'd be taking the kids to school and asked if I could please give them a ride to school, too. Nothing beat the education that those women gave our children, with their hearts and with their souls. They were truly dedicated and taught our children right from wrong in the correct manner and with love. That was the best education that anyone could have ever gotten.

My friend, Deanna Ostrawski was Bonnie's home economics teacher in junior high school. We were friends for many years and had lunch together often. We would discuss the quality of education that was offered to students at the Turtle Creek Schools at that time and we always agreed that it was unparalleled.

After the passing of my grandmother in 1954, my mother's family remained very close. My mother and her sisters talked on the phone daily and often got together for lunch or coffee. Family functions were held frequently and everyone was always included, even all of the cousins. On holidays, everyone visited everyone. Doors were always open and the table was always set. Each one of my mother's sisters had a specialty and many of them had more than one. Aunt Jean was known for her filled cookies and her pita, which was fruit pastry. Uncle Charlie's wife, Aunt Mary made the best bread and was an exquisite seamstress. Aunt Irene Piazza was known for biscotti Italian cookies and her wine jelly. Aunt Dorothy Rapp was known for her rosettes, her home-made candies, and her abilities as a seamstress. Aunt Edna Sikora was an excellent baker and made the best sea foam candy, and stuffed cabbage. Aunt Betty Evancho makes the best pierogie and chicken soup with home-made noodles. My mother made nut roll, paczkis, and krusciki. All of these things were shared with everyone and served at nearly every family event. Traditions of making these delicacies were and are kept sacred within the family to this day.

It was decided by my mother's youngest brother, Warren, that he would host family reunions. He owned a large farm and sportsman's lodge near Fort Necessity, the ideal place to have it. Usually there were over one hundred in attendance. He had horseback riding, a swimming pool, a fishing lake, and many activities for everyone to do. There was always a big hayride, and a family softball game. They would use cow pies to mark the bases. YUK! It was a fun-filled event that ended with a large delicious barbecue supper. Everyone brought one of their specialties to share. We all had wonderful memories of all of these family events. It was Uncle Warren that continued to go from house to house as the "family Santa" and he would always remember to stop at our house. As the kids got older, they would ask why Santa smells like cigars.

We always had fun with Halloween. We would take the kids to Hohmann's market or to Kubrick's farm market to pick out pumpkins. Walter enjoyed carving them and decorating the front porch with them. Many of the adults enjoyed dressing up. Aunt Betty and Mrs. Muir usually would and I remember that one year they were dressed as witches. Walter liked to get in on it, too. One year, he and Anna Mae Rustic, and Irene's Joey dressed up and went out to have some fun. My mother's sister Jean and her husband Andrew Shogan had a small neighborhood store down on Maple Avenue. They decided to go there to see if they would be recognized by them. Walter was dressed up as Frankenstein, Joey was a hobo, and Anna Mae had on another costume. They went into Aunt Jean's store and everyone fell silent. They started walking around then went and stood directly in front of Aunt Jean and Uncle Andy at the counter. No one said a word. Uncle Andrew handed them each a bag and told them to help themselves with the candy counter, but he was obviously quite shaken by their presence. They were scared to death and thought that these Halloween visitors were there to rob them! Aunt Jean started to reach for the phone, and then everyone took off their masks. It's a wonder that they didn't give them a heart attack. They very well could have gotten arrested. Everyone laughed and laughed and never forgot that Halloween night. My children always had a good time on Halloween night going trick or treating. They would each take a pillowcase for their candy and usually they had enough to last until Christmas. I never had to worry about the houses that they went to or the treats that they got. Louise always made the kids, red candied apples and they were so good. It was completely safe and very enjoyable.

In 1958, Irene had back surgery and she was going to have a long recovery. Things were not going well for them and they were not able to keep their house in Fairhaven Heights. They decided to move in with my parents along with their boys and their dog, Smokey. Once again, my parent's house was a very active place. My mother and father were there to lend a hand. My mother was used to having people stop by every day. There was always someone, a neighbor, a friend or family member who stopped by to chat or have a cup of coffee. There was always someone sitting at the kitchen table. My mother made coffee every morning in a thirty six cup electric party style coffee urn. It would be drained empty by seven o'clock that evening.

Life continued in its same routine. I followed the rules taught by my mother. On Mondays, we did the laundry. I got my first automatic clothes dryer when we first moved into the house, which was a real nightmare. It was an electric Speed Queen that we bought at Kelly and Cohen in Monroeville. Every time I would use it, a shower of sparks would fly from out of the back and it would pop and blow fuses! I was scared to death of it and continued to rely on the clothesline. I could always hear Louise in her basement when she washed. She had an old Thor wringer washer and as the clothes would agitate, the washer would "walk" across the floor, to a point that it would eventually unplug from the outlet and simply become stuck. Then, the electric cord would no longer reach the outlet to be plugged back in. Being so small and petite, it was a struggle for Louise to move it back to finish washing. I usually heard a string of profanity as she would eventually get it moved closer to the outlet. Tuesday was ironing day, but I would dampen the clothes the night before by sprinkling them with water. On Wednesday, windows were washed. Thursday, bedclothes and towels were washed and the upstairs bedrooms were cleaned. Mattresses were turned and vacuumed regularly. The children made their beds every morning from the time they were toddlers, without being told to do so. Friday, we cleaned downstairs thoroughly. The house would be filled with the wonderful scent of cedar from the O'Cedar's furniture polish that came in the red glass bottle. Our Hoover upright made short work of thoroughly vacuuming the carpets, but the Electrolux was used on upholstered furniture, stairs and to reach under the beds and furniture. The kitchen floor was scrubbed then waxed thoroughly by getting on your hands and knees. The children always helped me. I would give each of them dust-cloths to use and then they would sit on the Electrolux and I would pull them along as I vacuumed. I was teaching them and our home was always company ready. It was just as my mother taught us to do.

My mother with her brothers and sisters in 1959.

On Thursday, in the morning, I would usually take the car and go to do the grocery shopping. I would start by going to Turtle Creek, sometimes going to the bank and post office. When the kids were not in school, they would go with me and we always had a good time. Irene came along and did her shopping, too. We went to Ferri's market where they would have sawdust on the floor. I usually went to the Liberty Market as I liked their fresh produce and I knew Helen, Betty, and Pearl who worked there. We stopped by Nils Bakery for some baked goods. They had the best decorated cookies and frosted sponge cakes. After that, it was off to the Five and Ten. That was one of our favorite places and I could find just about anything there. Over the years, I knew many of the girls who worked there. When Kenny was small, he was like a little social ambassador. Everyone would stop and talk to him and everyone knew him. One cold, dark Christmas Eve, in the middle of a snow storm, Dorothy Irwin, a girl who worked in the store, walked all of the way to our house to bring him a little gift. It was well over a mile. We'd always run into Daisy Snyder, who was usually doing her shopping that day and she would always say, "How's my Kenny, today?" He was Mr. Popularity alright. That old five and ten truly was a special place. There were the old wooden floors and old ceiling fans that would wobble. The display cases were the same ones that were there when I was a small girl. The candy counter was just incredible!

We then drove up to the top of the hill in North Versailles where they had just opened a new A&P grocery store. That is where we did the rest of the grocery shopping. I always ran into someone that I knew there, too. Once Kenny was old enough, I taught him how to order the coffee from Burt who worked the coffee grinder and coffee counter. He would go up to him and say "A pound of Eight O'clock ground for perk, please." It was cute and Burt would always smile. The coffee smelled so good. I still use that brand today as well as an old electric percolator.

I was the one who usually drove on shopping day as our Chevy was a station wagon. Irene drove their turquoise and white '58 Chevy sometimes. It was really a squeeze though when Jack traded that car for a brand-new red Corvair. Once in a while a neighbor, Evelyn, who lived down the street from us, would ask to tag along with us to the A&P. Irene and I would always wonder what they ever ate as all she bought were paper products. Saturdays were still family shopping days. We would often go into downtown Pittsburgh and go to the big department stores. The kids liked to ride on the escalators, especially the old wooden ones that were still used on the upper floors. Once, I had on a pair of the new style narrow stiletto high heels and as we were getting off one of the escalators, it took the shoe right off of my foot and proceeded to "eat" the heel. We were immediately approached by one of the floor supervisors and he took us to the ladies shoe department, where I selected a new pair of shoes at no charge. Talk about customer service. Today, that would be unheard of. There was W.T. Grant's five and ten that was three floors high. The kids loved that as they had a huge toy department. On payday, each child picked one small toy, if he or she had been good, so they were always in their glory. We would go to Donohue's or get hot roast beef sandwiches at Dutch Henry's by Market Square.

Many times, we found ourselves going to Braddock to shop and then stopping at Sadowski's electric and hardware store, and then Och's for baked goods. We often went to McKeesport. There was another large five and ten store there called Green's, that the kids enjoyed. There we went to Balsamo's market and bakery. We loved to get their fresh whipped cream cakes for only 98 cents!

Kenny enjoying an "All-Day Sucker" on our swing in 1960.

Of course, we would always stop at National Record Mart and buy the records that we liked. The kids always picked out the latest 45's and couldn't wait to go home to play them. There were many nice stores like Cox's, Jaison's, and a big Sears Roebuck department store. Walter liked Henry B. Klein's for men. We stopped at the L&B for supper on the way home. They had great burgers and shakes, not to mention a jukebox. We always had dinner out on Saturday and it was a real treat. Occasionally, we would go to Cole's Corner restaurant in Monroeville. The children really enjoyed Eat-N-Park when they opened on Route 22, with their carhop service and Big-Boy hamburgers.

In 1956, Miracle Mile shopping center opened up and we went there often. There was a grocery store I liked called Star Market that was later called Loblaw's. There were two five and ten stores and a big Sun Drugstore. In the summer, they always sold snow cones outside of Woolworth's. Many times, Louise and I drove out there in her pink Studebaker, to shop and walk around. Ronnie's first official job was at a children's clothing store there called "Young Fashions." Irene worked there for a short time. Louise worked at Miracle Mile briefly at a shop called "Gaylord's" and I worked also there at a ladies clothing store called "The Darling Shop." Ronnie started doing our lawn and yard work as he was growing up. He kept everything impeccably manicured and the front lawn was always beautiful. He started helping a neighbor, Bob, who lived up the street. Bob paid him and that taught him about earning spending money. In fact, a few months before he was even sixteen, he had already bought his first car, a Studebaker Hawk. I swear he would wash and polish it every day until he could finally drive it. Sometimes, he wanted me to drive him to school in it. He got his driver's license and started working for Mel Pollock at "Young Fashions" after school and on weekends.

Walter traded the Chevy on a white 1960 Pontiac. It was a very stylish, beautiful car, and the size of an aircraft carrier. It had power everything including brakes, which I wasn't used to. Every morning, the kids would climb in and I would drive them to school. At the end of Mercer Street, I would make a sharp left turn out onto James Street. As I would do this, the car would stall. I would tap my foot on the big chrome brake pedal and it would go completely to the floor and the car would keep going down the hill. Once the car stalled, the brakes did not work. I would usually just panic. I used the parking brake to finally stop the car and jam the gear shift into park and try to start the car again. The kids thought it was funny as heck as they would slide around on the leather seats and laugh as I frantically tried to stop the car. I didn't think it was so funny and neither did Walter. He took the car back to where he bought it in Monroeville several times, to have the problem fixed, but it continued to do the same thing. One day he and Brownie took the car back out there and I could not believe what he did. He aimed the nose of the Pontiac directly at the big glass window of the showroom, hopped the curb with the two front wheels and stopped inches before the grill was touching the glass. He and Brownie got out of the car and he went inside and got the salesman by the shirt collar and said "Today, you'll do something about that car, or it's coming through the glass, back into the showroom!" The salesman looked around and saw where the car was and he was absolutely horrified. Walter and Brownie returned a short time later with another 1960 Pontiac. This one was green and it didn't stall once.

Rusty loved the kids, but was especially protective of baby Kenny. All you had to do was to say to him "I'm going to hit the baby" and he would start growling, snarling, baring his teeth at you. When Kenny was small, Rusty would grab him by his pant legs and drag him all around the kitchen table. Kenny would laugh and laugh.

My parents and their grandchildren on Easter, 1960.

Once I got a very disturbing phone call from an older woman on James Street telling me Rusty was doing his business in her yard, as he would romp about all over Electric Plan. She was not nice and I didn't want trouble from her, so I took Rusty to the dog pound. I was so upset. Irene came over and I was crying and crying, as I was scrubbing the kitchen floor on my hands and knees. We got in the car and drove back to the pound and brought him home. He was more than a member of our family, he was like another child.

Rusty would roam all over the hill known as Electric Plan. I often wonder how many puppies he fathered and wish I had one of his ancestors today. Many times, Ernie Rubash would call me from the Mobile gas station. He would say, "Maryann, I've got Rusty down here. Could you come down and pick him up because I don't want him to get hit by a car on James Street." I drove down and when Rusty would see me his tail would start wagging. Ernie would have him in the office until I got there. I would always thank Ernie, as that was a very nice thing to do. Rusty knew exactly where my parents lived and would visit them at their house when he was out and about. He would scratch at the door and they would let him in to say hello. He would go directly to the refrigerator and sit and stare at it and bark. My mother thought he had not eaten but that wasn't the case at all. She or my father cut up three hot dogs and feed them to him. Then he'd leave and come home. This routine got to be a habit that went on for a long time. My mother started to write a note and put it under his collar. The note would say "I was at Grandma's and ate three hot dogs." Sometimes my mother would phone to say Rusty was there and had just left. Shortly, I would see him running down the back path and hopping Louise's back fence like a reindeer. He would come into the kitchen and let us see the note. Once, Mr. Wetzig, who lived behind us on Locust Street, stopped to pet Rusty and saw and read the note. He was hysterical and called me on the phone laughing about it. He was really some dog!

Walter was very happy when the kids were old enough to do the lawn and keep the hedges shaped and manicured. It was a real treat for the boys as they could use the power lawn mower and that made them feel grown up. Walter wasn't one for doing most things around the house. He loved to wash and polish the cars. The garage always smelled of Simonize and chrome polish. I had a bad time with backing the car out of the driveway. Those stone walls seemed to get closer as I would inch out backwards. If Walter was at work and I needed to get the car out, I'd ask Brownie. If Brownie wasn't home, I'd get Louise to help direct me. She had troubles of her own. She had a blue '54 Ford that she could never get started. It had a manual choke and she would flood the engine every time. That was easy to solve. She waited for the mailman, Jim Woods, who was able to start that Ford on the first try. The Ford eventually turned into a pink '59 Studebaker Lark. Brownie also had a '55 Cadillac and it was a sight to see Louise driving that car. She could hardly see over the big steering wheel and all you could see was her hairdo and bright red fingernails clutching the steering wheel. We had so much fun together and a lot of laughs.

If Walter wasn't doing the car, I would find him in the basement fooling with electronics or doing television repair. He built a complete home entertainment section into a wall in our basement game room. It was complete with television, turntable, stereo, and several speakers. He went a little crazy the year that "Stereo" came out and had speakers everywhere. Walter was not one to help around the house. The kids and I did all of the painting without his help, as he was a sloppy painter. We remember him balancing precariously on a high ladder, installing the heavy wooden storm windows every fall, before the coming of cold winter weather. They helped with insulating those old metal casement style windows from the howling winter wind. Then, every spring, he would have to un-install those heavy storm windows until the next year. He wasn't much for helping me with the housework either. Once, he ran my Electrolux vacuum and did nothing but nick up the baseboards with the metal rug nozzle and knock things over with the hose. He never vacuumed again. Walter made eggs or sometimes, pancakes for weekend breakfasts, and was capable of using the barbecue grill. Once, he told Kenny that they were going to bake me a cake. They got the batter all mixed up and into the cake pans. Walter went to set the dial on the oven and the oven control knob shot off the oven, and flew across the kitchen. OOPS! A few days later, I had a beautiful new Gallery style range with double ovens and that was worth it to me.

Our home was always open to the children's friends. Ronnie and his friends, Billy Depner, Bobby Mameaux, and Johnny Jessup would be in my kitchen making pizza, frying donuts, or up in his bedroom playing records. Once he was driving, they would go to the movies. Jeanne Lewandowski would come down the path with a little pink suitcase, to come and stay overnight and play with Bonnie. They played together since they were babies. Beverly Jones would come over to play with Bonnie, too. They played with her dolls or board games. Sometimes, they watched American Bandstand on television or made fudge. Beverly even accompanied us on a summer vacation to the Jersey shore. They got along great and Beverly was very well behaved with good manners.

When Kenny was small, his playmate was Jeffrey Dudley who lived two houses up the street. In 1959, my cousin Anthony Rustic, his wife Anna Mae and their children moved to a new house that they had built near us on George Street. They had been living with Anthony's mother, my Aunt Vic, on Summit Street in Braddock. Every time they would drive by, they always would stop and say hello when we were outside. On occasion, Anna Mae would stop by for a cup of coffee. Their youngest daughter, Michelle, was a year older than Kenny and would come over to play. I would ask her what she would like to eat and she would say "mayonnaise bread or creamed corn." She was a sweet little girl and played nicely with Kenny. Cousins were playing together just as we had done as children.

My father's sister, Helena (Lena), came back to live in the United States from Poland. She lived there for nearly fifty years and had been through so much. She moved to Braddock to live with her daughter, Maria and her husband who had been in the prison camps. Aunt Lena was very sweet and we all got to know and enjoy her. She always told us that she remembered her older sisters going ice skating on the frozen Susquehanna River when they lived in Steelton, before moving to Braddock. So much history and so many family stories were lost when that generation passed on.

The decade of the 1950s was such a wonderful time for us. Lives were much simpler and people valued good ethics and morals. Our family and extended family were very strong and shared immeasurable love for one another. We enjoyed many family celebrations parties and events together. Turtle Creek provided such a strong sense of community and our neighborhood on Electric Plan gave us comfort, security, and many wonderful times. We had simple pleasures and simple fun. Music, television and entertainment in general provided for quality time together that was much more satisfying and appreciated. Our family was young and there were so many things that would lie ahead for them. Promising futures were on the horizon, but they still had time to enjoy their youth for a little while longer and so could we.

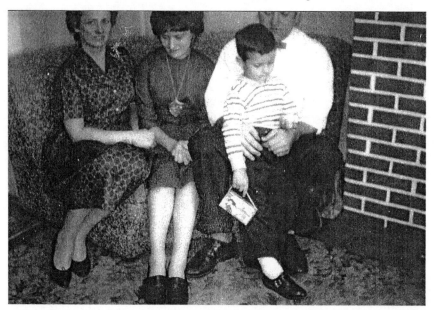

Bonnie, Walter, Kenny, and me in 1962.

Maturity and Grandchildren

The decade of the 1960s brought many changes to our lives as well as the world. Some of the changes were good, some were not. Time marches on.

Irene's oldest son, Jackie, graduated from high school in 1960 and enlisted in the Navy. My father was very proud of that as he loved the Navy so much. Irene started working part-time at Esman's in Turtle Creek. It was a sporting goods shop that also sold toys. Irene eventually found herself working in the office at Sears and Roebuck in East Liberty, with my friend, Louise Brown. Irene did collections and I'm sure that she did a good job and didn't let too many get away.

My father had his stroke in May of 1961 and his recovery was not too good. It really affected his quality of life. Within a short time after that, his brother Eddie passed away from cancer and Stacia went to live with Aunt Ceil in Braddock.

Uncle John had been living near South Park and was becoming frail and getting ill. He had gotten tuberculosis during one of his tours of duty while in the Navy. It was catching up with him and he wasn't doing well. He left Pittsburgh and moved into a U.S. Naval retirement home that was on Grey's Ferry Road in Philadelphia. It was a beautiful place and he was very happy there. He would often fly to Pittsburgh to visit us and my children remember trips to the Greater Pittsburgh Airport to pick him up and take him back. He would always fly on TWA and we would watch his plane take off from the gate outside at the airport. He would wave to us from the window as the plane would taxi away. Uncle John's health continued to decline and he passed away in 1963.

Ronnie graduated from high school in May of 1962. We were very proud of him as he was an honor roll student and graduated in the top of his class. He worked at small department store called Jaffee's in Butler and started to attend college at night. He did that for a short time and then went to the drafting department in the generator division at the Westinghouse plant in East Pittsburgh. He continued to pursue college courses at night as he had much bigger plans for his future. After twelve years of employment at Westinghouse, Ronnie moved west to Las Vegas, Nevada to pursue his dreams!

Bonnie also did very well in school and was well liked by all of her teachers. She always expressed an interest in Art even from a very early age. When she was a little girl, she loved to draw, paint, and color and would sit for hours doing so. She won an art contest on a local children's television show called "Ricky and Copper" and her prize was a huge box of Crayola crayons that the studio delivered to our house. She was thrilled! When she was in junior high school, she was asked to attend special art classes that were offered in Oakland. The classes were held on Saturday and were only offered to above average art students that showed exceptional talent. Uncle John bought Bonnie a professional easel and a Jon Nagy artist set. It was complete with tubes of paint in many colors, brushes and pallet. The kit had all of the tools that a professional artist would use. She really started to show how very artistically talented she was. While in high school, Bonnie had brief employment at the Sun Drug store on Penn Avenue in Turtle Creek. She was such a great help to me, not only with the house, but with watching Kenny as I was working at the time for Gimbels, to help save for her college expenses. I always appreciated her help around the house.

She also graduated near the top of her class in Turtle Creek high school in May of 1966. She received two scholarships to a private girl's college in Oakland, called Mount Mercy. The college was later renamed Carlow College. She would commute by bus most of the time and on occasion, we would drive in to the city and pick her up if she was staying later. For a while she would ride with Billy Evancho, Aunt Betty's son, who was then attending the University of Pittsburgh. During the summer, Bonnie worked with the summer arts and crafts program at the schools in Turtle Creek. She did that for a couple of years and really enjoyed it. This experience only confirmed her desire to be an art teacher. She was very dedicated to her studies and in her senior year, she had an art show of her work at the college. We were very proud of her and her talents!

Kenny was also very well behaved and a good student while attending Electric Plan school. He enjoyed the teachers that he had and they enjoyed him. He would sometimes go to my parent's house for lunch and after school. My father was not doing too well by then and that gave him something to look forward to when Kenny would go there for lunch. My father would tell the stories of his youth and Kenny would intently listen. They both enjoyed that time together.

Once, Kenny pestered us for a pet snake, of all things. A man that worked with Ronnie caught a very small one in his yard and sent it home with Ronnie in a mason jar and Kenny loved it. It wasn't so bad when the snake was small but it grew quickly and was starting to bite when you would handle it. Ronnie and Kenny took it down to the creek in Linhart and set it free, so he got that out of his system. Kenny graduated from Turtle Creek high school in 1976 and immediately started at the University of Pittsburgh and he hated it. He left college and started to work as an optician and still works in the optical field today.

In 1963, Gimbels department store opened its first suburban location at a new state of the art designed shopping center, called Eastland in North Versailles. Eastland was the first of its kind to feature an outdoor shopping area, as well as an indoor mall shopping area. It was way ahead of its time. I began working there for Gimbels, part-time and loved it. Anna Mae Rustic also worked there and we would occasionally share rides when our schedules would allow it. I worked there for three years until my father's health really began to decline and I was needed more at home. I ended up going back to work for Gimbels at their Monroeville Mall location in 1973 and loved it. It was there that I got to meet Ruth Handler, the owner of Mattel and inventor of the "Barbie" doll, when she came to introduce a mastectomy prosthesis, that I learned how to fit. I also had the pleasure of meeting Gloria Vanderbilt when she came to our store to promote her merchandise. I had the honor of being chosen to go to speak at the Penn State Extention Campus, on the topic of "Proper Business Attire". I enjoyed giving the lecture and was very well received. I had a total of twenty eight years with them, when I retired as "Head of Sales" when Gimbels closed all of its locations in the late 1980s. I enjoyed my job and made many wonderful friends that I still have today.

We continued to vacation every year, but not just to the Jersey shore. We found our way west and had many wonderful experiences on old Route 66. I think that the kids learned more on old Route 66 than they did all year in school. We fell in love with the desert and its natural beauty and with the southwest. We enjoyed the excitement of Las Vegas, Nevada and Walter was in his glory with the gambling and the night life! We always said that we would retire to a warm place in the west and often thought it would be Las Vegas. Other years saw other trips to other places. Florida, California, Canada, Mexico, New England, and the Carolinas, were among many of our travels that we all enjoyed. My last trip was to London, England a couple of years ago.

This country of ours is a beautiful and fascinating place. Everyone should experience its beauty and the nice people that you cross paths with, as you travel through the little towns along the way. All of these experiences leave imprints on your mind and on your soul, and stay with you all through your life.

Life had really changed for my parents, as it sometimes does during retirement years. One never knows what can lie ahead. My father's health declined with each passing year. He enjoyed being in his home and everyone tried to make his life as pleasurable as possible. My parents still had a lot of visitors and that occupied my father. Helen and Frank Palmer would visit from next door, on the back porch in good weather. Lucille Turk and Rosie Hlavety would walk over to visit. Rosie worked with my mother when she wound coils on the production floor at Westinghouse, and they remained friends and talked nearly every day. Rosie would play cards with my mother and did so until my mother passed away years later. She remained a spinster all of her life.

Aunt Jean's husband, Uncle Andy would stop by in the evening several nights each week to sit and visit with my father. He always brought him a pack of cigarettes and they would sit and smoke and talk for hours of the fun they had in days gone by. My father looked forward to Uncle Andy's visits as they were quite close all of their married lives. They were both a lot of fun in their younger days. Uncle Andy would show up faithfully, even in bad weather. If the sidewalks were slippery with ice, Uncle Andy would take off his shoes and walk carefully in his socks. Every time Uncle Andy's face would appear in the window of the kitchen door, my father's face would light up!

Often Aunt Edna and Uncle Steve would come and visit for the evening. Aunt Edna was very sweet and kind and Uncle Steve was full of interesting stories. They lived in Turtle Creek on Watson Drive in the Electric Heights Housing project all of their lives. Uncle Steve would sometimes bring his projector and show movies. That was his hobby and everyone in the family enjoyed his movies.

Once in a while, when my father was still able to get out of the house, Anna Mae Rustic would call and say "Uncle Joe…..Get your coat on….I'll pick you up in ten minutes!" Before her car would come down the alley, my father would be waiting by the back gate. She would take him to Carl's Tavern in Braddock, where they would share a pitcher of beer with a double shot of whiskey, called a "clucker". He loved that!

One summer, while we were in route from Las Vegas to Los Angeles, my father fell down the basement stairs and broke his hip. Upon arriving at Herkie's home in Thousand Oaks, we had a message from Irene. Walter put the kids and me on a plane for Pittsburgh. That marked the beginning of the end, for my poor father. His health rapidly deteriorated from that point and he never quite recovered. He was only home for a brief time. I'll always remember the kindness of John Sapida, going in to his drug store, to make a prescription up for my father in the middle of the night. He then, delivered it to my parent's door on his way back home. How can you ever forget such kindness? That's exactly what made Turtle Creek the kind of town that it was!

Doctor Pollock would come up to check on my father and when he was about to leave, he would sit down at the kitchen table for a cup of coffee. My mother would ask how much she would owe him for his visit and he would say "Oh Helen… Just make me some of your good lentil soup." Dr. Harry Pollock practiced medicine in Turtle Creek for many years. In fact, he shared a waiting room with his friend, Dr. Allan, the dentist, on the second floor of a building on Penn Avenue. Dr. Pollock had lost an arm because of radiation burns from not using the lead-lined gloves, while taking x-rays with his own equipment. Afterward, he continued to practice and make house calls, even driving himself. The kindness of these professionals helped many in our community. No one was ever turned away or refused of their professional help because of the inability to pay for services. It was real dedication. Not just to their profession, but to humanity. You just don't find that people would do that sort of thing, in today's world and that makes me sad.

It was at a point that my father could no longer be cared for at home. He went to a nursing facility in Oakland on Forbes Avenue and my mother would visit him every day. It was true devotion. Irene and I would take turns driving her into Oakland and picking her up after she saw that he had his meals and was taken care of. Sometimes, it would coincide with Bonnie's class schedule at college and trips could be consolidated. I continued to drive and at least made one trip a day into Oakland. I took turns driving my mother each way, even driving on my share of snowy and icy roads, but my mother spent every day with my father. It was true dedication, but exhausting.

There was no choice now, that my mother was going to have to sell their home to help pay for my father's care. Their savings was starting to really dwindle, and my father now required nursing care. The house that my parents built together at 612 Locust Street, and turned into a warm and loving home for us, had to be sold. It saddened all of us greatly, but there was no choice. In the summer of 1969, the house was sold and our lives changed again. Irene and Jack moved to an apartment in Monroeville for a short time and ended up moving to 83-C Harper Drive in the Electric Heights Housing project. At one point, we all lived on Harper Drive, in "the Project". It was their turn.

My mother came and stayed with us for a while. My father was moved to another nursing facility on Upper Fifth Avenue. He was given the best of care and spent the last few months of his life, in the company of Pittsburgh's most prominent attorneys and professionals and the daughter of one of the owners of Pittsburgh's largest steel mill.

Our phone rang in the middle of the night and we all knew exactly what it was. My father passed away on January 13th, 1970. On May 17th of that year, he would have been 75 years old.

My mother had decided to move to Aunt Jean's house on Cedar Avenue. Her children had all gone and the second floor of her nine room house was completely empty. In fact it was only Aunt Jean and Uncle Andy, all alone in the entire house. My mother enjoyed their companionship. Every night while Aunt Jean was still working at her little store on Maple Avenue, Uncle Andy and my mother would enjoy a big soup bowl full of ice cream, while watching Redd Foxx on television.

My mother enjoyed her years that she spent on Cedar Avenue. She was back in her old neighborhood and back in a house that my father had actually built. Aunt Jean's house was a busy place, just as our house once was, so there was always activity there for her. Her friends would always go to visit her and Rosie still went over to play cards and have lunch.

My mother still cooked and baked. In fact, she continued to make the nut roll and prune roll for the Holidays. Aunt Jean had a large Weimaraner dog, named "Hans". He was very sweet and loved my mother and knew exactly where her cookie jar was! He spent a lot of time in my mother's kitchen and was company for her. My mother spent an entire day baking nut roll and prune roll for everyone for the holidays and her kitchen counters were lined with loaves of bread that were still cooling. When my mother wasn't looking, Hans came into the kitchen and sampled nearly every loaf! My mother couldn't possibly be angry with Hans as he was her pal and we always laugh about that every time we make nut roll.

Kenny spent every Saturday morning visiting his Grandma and that was their special time. She would always have fresh Snickerdoodle cookies and they would sit and visit. He would get groceries that she needed and do little chores for her. She would always tell stories about growing up and loved to talk about her life.

Sadly, my mother passed away on March 24th, 1977, at seventy six years of age. We still miss her, greatly.

We lost our beloved Rusty in January of 1971. He had developed cancer and had to be put to sleep. He was 14 years old and had a happy and charmed life. He was a member of our family, just as all of our dogs would be, and his loss was difficult. We got our first Scottish terrier in April of that year, from a breeder in Salisbury, Missouri. His name was MacDuff, but we called him "Duffy". He was a typical Scotty with the Scotty attitude. He was a show quality dog but we did not show him. He was his own dog and was very protective. When all of us were at work and school and Duffy was home alone, he would climb up on the top of our loveseat in front of our front window and watch everything that went on up and down Mercer Street. Walter would take him to Monroeville Mall and walk him on his leash while he waited for me to finish working, when he would pick me up. He was not quite ten years old and developed cancer and had to be put to sleep.

Our next dog was another Scotty that we named Holly. She was born in the nursery at the Animal Rescue League and was given to me right before my birthday in 1981, by Kenny and Bonnie's husband, Jim. She was a very smart dog and loved to play ball with Walter. She loved to sit at the top of the stairs and Walter would be at the bottom. He would throw the ball up to her and she would catch it and then drop it back down the stairs for him to catch. That was one of her favorite pastimes. We would tell her that it was almost bedtime and to pick up her toys and she actually would! She'd put them in a basket where we kept them by the fireplace. She also lived to be fourteen years old, when we had to have Dr. Shrader put her to sleep.

Our home on Mercer Street in 1969.

Daisy was our next Scotty pup. She was just like a child to us and very smart, just as our other dogs had been. Walter and I both were very close to her and she was really a sweet dog. Walter and Daisy ate breakfast together every morning! Then, they would go to the patio and Daisy would sit with him while he read the morning paper. She moved to Las Vegas with us when she just over a year old.

When Walter passed away, Daisy would lay in the hallway each morning outside of the bedroom door, like she was waiting for him and their morning routine. It took her a long time to mourn his passing, and then she became very attached to me. We lost her to cancer in September of 2008.

Now there is a new Scotty pup named Maggie. She came to live with us on the day after Thanksgiving in 2008. She's grown to be just the same as our other Scotties were. They were all sweet little dogs, and wonderful companions and members of our family. Our philosophy was always that our dogs were just like our children and we treated them the very same way. If you don't give them the proper attention, your love and the best of care, then you should not have them. We always felt that way and perhaps that's why our dogs were always so intelligent and so devoted to us.

Walter continued to take Kenny on fishing trips. They would usually go to Keystone State Park, Mountain Valley, or to Twin Lakes near Greensburg. Walter was getting older but still had a few crazy moments. He brought home a big, black Pontiac Bonneville one time. It had a big 455 Cadillac engine. He told Kenny to get in as they were going to take it down on the Tri-Boro highway to "see what it could do!" but he then added, "but don't tell your Mother!"

Walter always refused to wear blue jeans. When he was growing up, only poor kids would wear blue jeans and tennis shoes. He always wore dress slacks and even khakis were a push for him. Even when we dated, he would wear white dress shirts and ties. In the seventies, he loved what they would call "leisure suits" and had many of them. They were pants with matching jackets that you would wear with brightly colored floral shirts, and of course patent leather shoes. He just thought that was so spiffy! Thank heavens that trend faded and he went back to much more conservative ties and blazers. Even in his retirement years, he would wear shirts and ties to run errands and to go to the grocery store.

Walter always enjoyed gambling and he was a risk taker. We would go to the harness racing track at the Meadows, south of Pittsburgh, for dinner and an evening out on occasion. Sometimes, my friend Teddy, her husband, Cab and Irene and Jack would go with us. We would have a lot of fun and it was a nice evening out. Walter enjoyed playing the illegal numbers game. He would even place bets for my grandmother, my mother and a couple of her friends. He knew where to go, and he knew the bookies in the valley. He was never that lucky, but just the thrill of gambling and chance, excited him. When Pennsylvania started the state lottery, he really enjoyed that and would play and follow it daily.

In fact, once he was retired and wasn't working, he and a group of his buddies would meet every day for coffee and conversation. Usually, they would meet at a restaurant or in the food court at Monroeville Mall. He knew many of them for years from the valley, and some were businessmen from Monroeville. They would discuss current events and analyze the lottery and the numbers game. They had a lot of fun together and it was their daily social routine. If it was one of their birthdays, I would bake a cake for them and he would take it with him. They really enjoyed their friendship and had a good time. I always referred to them as the "Sunshine Boys".

Walter retired from the Westinghouse plant on January 1st, 1984, at age 62. He had started working for Westinghouse on May 14th, 1941, so he had 43 years service with them. I guess by today's standard, longevity of employment like that is unheard of. So many people then dedicated their entire lives to those companies and corporations. Upon his retirement, Westinghouse presented him with an engraved mug. After a short while, Walter went back to work. He worked for Schwab Metal Spinning Company and then, as a consultant for an engineering firm, doing work for Duquesne Light Company. He enjoyed his work and was never lazy.

One of the momentous occasions in our life was the marriage of our Bonnie. She married James Matta on July 29th, 1978. We gave her an elegant formal wedding with all of the trimmings and it was a major celebration in our lives. The candlelight ceremony was held at the Heinz Memorial Chapel on Fifth Avenue in Oakland at seven thirty in the evening. Everything was simply beautiful. A dinner reception was held immediately following the ceremony, at the Holiday House supper club in Monroeville. It truly was a grand evening that I'll never forget.

Aaronell Shaila Matta was born on March 23rd, 1983 in Calcutta, India. She is our first grandchild and only granddaughter. What a beautiful baby girl she was, and what a joy to all of our lives! She arrived on a special day about eight weeks after she was born. A volunteer that worked for Air Mexico made the trip with our dear baby, Aaronell. They flew through Germany and France and it took nearly twenty four hours, with the stops that they made. Our first grandchild! What a thrill! All of us shared in the excitement and joy.

Zachary Krishnan Matta was born on September 23rd, 1985, in a mission in Northern India. We had been waiting for a brother for our Aaronell and again, we celebrated the joy and excitement of our first and only grandson! He arrived in Pittsburgh in late November. A volunteer travelled with him on his long journey, but they came around the globe in the other direction, from west to east. He was so small and so cute and had a head of black curly hair. Poor Aaronell wasn't thrilled as she was expecting a brother that was her size, not a baby. She wanted to send him back!

Oh, what fun we had with our grandchildren! Now, I know the joy that my parents experienced with their grandchildren and I loved every minute of it. We attended many violin concerts, plays and school functions. We enjoyed our Holiday celebrations and Birthdays with the children and will always have special memories of those times. Walter had a Santa Suit and would make surprise visits every year to instill the magic of Christmas and Santa Claus. Yes, he was the one in the Santa suit wandering along Harrison City road! He just loved doing that and did it for a few years before the children would become wise.

Thirty four years after we bought our house at 658 Mercer Street, on the hill known as Electric Plan, we sold it and moved into a new townhouse in the little town of Trafford. There, we were closer to our grandchildren and it was time to move on to a new chapter in our lives. Our house on Mercer Street saw many improvements through the years, and was much different than when we bought it in 1951. The neighborhood was just as nice as it was then, and people cared about the appearance of their homes. Turtle Creek was still a fine community.

Walter and me in 1990.

My grandchildren. Our future. Aaronell & Zachary Matta in 2008.

In September of 1992, Walter went in for routine surgery and afterward, had a stroke in the recovery room. His recovery was a long slow process and he was never quite the same. The kids were planning a surprise, catered party that November, to celebrate our 50th Wedding Anniversary, but it had to be cancelled.

Walter was in a rehabilitation hospital until mid-December. He recovered fairly well and eventually was able to get back his driver's license. After that, he had some good years and some that weren't so good.

In April of 1994, Irene got word that Jackie had passed away suddenly, while living on a ranch outside of Pocatello, Idaho. They were estranged and she had not seen him in a few years. He would have been 52 years old.

In 1995, I did the most difficult thing that I ever had to do. We moved from Pennsylvania to Las Vegas, Nevada. It was very difficult to leave Bonnie and my grandchildren, and the familiar places that I knew all of my life. At last, we were out in the West, in the nice warm sunshine.

Irene and Jack moved to North Carolina a couple years after we left Pennsylvania, to be near their grandchildren. Their health was starting to fail and the weather was milder for them. On February 16th, 2000, Irene passed away. Jack passed away a little over a year later.

Seven weeks before our 60th Wedding Anniversary, on September 22nd, 2002, Walter passed away from congestive heart failure. He enjoyed the last years of his life, and I really feel that our moving to Las Vegas and the warm climate, helped to extend his life and give him more happiness.

As I'm approaching the middle of my eighth decade, I now sit in the warm sunshine on the patio with Maggie and reflect. I find great comfort and enjoyment in these memories and will gladly share all of them with all of you that read this story. My life has been a rich, exciting adventure. The time of my childhood was so special to me, and those memories I hold very dear to my heart. It was magical! It truly was a special time and place to be; on a hill known as Electric Plan in the little town called Turtle Creek.

Epilogue

Well… Here it is… my story! This is a great accomplishment for me and I'm happy to share it with all who read it. I am neither rich nor famous. I'm just an ordinary person and mother to my children, who grew up during the trying times of the Great Depression. It was a time of many sacrifices and great hardships for our parents and grandparents. Everyone around us was in the same economic circumstance. Therefore, we never knew how poor we were. Being poor had nothing to do with having fun and creating our own pleasure and happiness. We enjoyed every day of our lives, with parents and grandparents who provided us with unconditional love. Everyone faces adversity in their lives, and it is the ability to deal with that adversity that makes you the type of person that you are. We are all responsible for our own destiny!

My parents taught us how important it was to be good people, and to be of good character. Integrity and your reputation follow you throughout your life, and it becomes one of your most valuable assets. We were taught not to be "followers", but to be "thinkers" and "leaders." These values were also instilled not only in me, but in my children.

To those of you who know us personally, it is easy to fill in the blanks and continue with this story. To those of you who don't know us, close your eyes and use your imagination. Life is a great mystery and no one knows what tomorrow can bring. Most times though, you must always remember that life will only be what you make of it.

Time is going by swiftly, and in the near future, people of my era will be gone. So will their stories and their history. One purpose of this book was to document my history and my story: to share it with all of you, and future generations that read this book. Events in our lives create memories. Those memories become stories. Those stories become our history. That time in my life, was a part of our history. It is very important to tell our own stories! My parents always said that "History is our greatest teacher," and that I truly believe. If we don't tell our stories, how will future generations learn about life at that time? How will our children learn about their heritage and their ancestors? These things are invaluable and must be preserved for future generations!

I was so fortunate to live my life when I did. I was so blessed to be born and grow up when, where, and how I did. Our youth is filled with so much hope and so many desires. I was young enough to experience youth with my children, and watch them grow into the adults that they are today. I'm very proud of them and who they have become! I look to my grandchildren, to continue on with the legacy of our family, its heritage, its devotion, closeness, and love.

Life has changed in so many ways over the years, and so have people. Many families have been scattered across miles and into the wind. There is not the bonding and the closeness, as there was before, and that is so very sad. I really hope that family values will change, and go back to the way they were before, when I was growing up.

Memories are very wonderful and powerful things! No one can ever take them from you. They are more precious than gold! My memories are still so fresh and palpable. If I close my eyes, I can still smell the delicious aromas coming from my mother's kitchen, hot coffee perking, and my father's Camel cigarettes. I can hear the sweet harmony of the Everly Brothers playing on our Hi-Fi, and the kids running down the path on their way home from school, and Louise calling from her kitchen window, "Maaarrryaaaannn, Whatcha doin'?" Whether it's holding my little grandbabies, watching the sun come through my kitchen window on Mercer Street, reading the kids a story, on a date in a booth with Walter eating ice cream at the Le Barbe, playing jacks with Irene on our back porch, or playing with my cousins along the "Indian Path," these trivial, little memories make us who we are!

This book is also a tribute to life in a small town and to the good people of Turtle Creek, whose lives once crossed paths with ours many years ago. It truly was a special place and I wonder just how many places like it exist today. Perhaps it's only in our memories.

I am both proud and privileged to tell my story to all of you. The story of my life and the story of my family will live on forever within the pages of this book. Telling my story has given me a purpose and has renewed by spirit. This has taken my life in a direction that I had never thought of until my eighth decade. I'm hopeful that my story leaves a positive impact with all of those who read it. Everyone has a story to tell and I hope this inspires all of you to do so. It proves that we are all capable of doing what we choose to do at any time or at any age.

I am very thankful for having such a wonderful family, living a long life, and having these beautiful memories to share with all of you, from days gone by, from the hill known as Electric Plan, in the little town called Turtle Creek.

Appendix

A. Family Genealogy

     The Krzyzosiak Family

     The Figulski Family

     The Sapp Family

     The Lawrence Family

B. List of my Memories

C. Recipes: My Mother's Specialties

     Helen Krzyzosiak's Krusciki (Polish Love Knots)

     Helen Krzyzosiak's Paczkis (Polish Filled Doughnuts)

APPENDIX A: *Family Genealogy*

Andrew Krzyzosiak (1850-1908)
Married
Emilie Bertha (Barbara) Sonnenberger (Sonnenberg) (1853-1905)

Children and their children:

<u>Anna</u> – Married Edward Symoroski
    Mary
    Stella
    Charles
    Leonard
    Agnes
    Edward

<u>Francis</u> – Married Walagorski (Wallace)
    Mayola
    Katherine
    Vincent
    Raymond & Edward (twins)

<u>Victoria</u> – Married Rustic (First Marriage)
    Rose
    Victoria
    Cecelia
    Stanley
    Edward
    Anthony
--Married Walter Przjynowski (Second Marriage)
    Anna
    Helen
    Laura
    Walter
    Anthony

<u>Max</u> – Married Anna Kupers
 Walter
 Max (Junior)
 Charles (Chuckie)
 John (Jack)

<u>Helena</u> (Lena) – Married Kazimier Rydarowski
 Maria
 Wanda
 Genu (Eugene)
 Stefcia

<u>Cecelia</u> (Ceil) – Married Frank Zygmunt
 Henry
 Matylda
 Theodore
 Leona
 Sylvia

<u>Valentina</u> (Stacia)

<u>John</u> – Married Florence Wiggins
 – Married Mae (Agnes) Christian

<u>Joseph</u> – Married Helen Figulski
 Irene
 Maryann (Me!)

<u>Edward</u>

Joseph Figulski (1867-1932)
Married
Marcianna Lewandowski (1878-1954)

Children and their Children:

Charles – Married Mary Panzchek
  Stanley
  Gregory
  Regina
  Gertrude (Trudy)
  Robert

Joseph – Married Anne Swersey
  Raymond
  Rita

Clinton – Married Victoria D.
  Robert

Helen – Married Joseph Krzyzosiak
  Irene
  Maryann (Me!)

Regina (Jean) – Married Andrew Shogan
  Marion
  Edward
  Andrew
  Dolores (Dolly)
  Joseph (Bob)
  Raymond & Ronald (twins)
  Patricia (Patty)
  Regis (Rege)

Irene – Married Gene D. Piazza

Dorothy – Married Albert Rapp

Edna – Married Stephen Sikora
  Stephen (Stevie)
  Donna
  Carol

<u>Elizabeth</u> (Betty) – Married Joseph Evancho
    Constance (Connie)
    Marjorie (Margie)
    Joseph (Billy)
    Marci

<u>Warren</u> – Married Mildred (Millie) Metcalf
    Judith (Judy)
    Warren
    Thomas
    Edward

Joseph Krzyzosiak
Married September 9, 1920
Helen Figulski

Children and their Children:

Irene - Married John Sapp
    John (Jackie) Sapp
        Jason
    Joseph (Joey) Sapp
        Michelle (Mimi) Richardson
        Joseph (J.D.) Richardson
        Jeremy Richardson
        Christopher
        Autumn

Maryann (Me!) - Married Walter Lawrence
    Ronald (Ronnie)
    Bonita (Bonnie) - Married James Matta
        Aaronell (Granddaughter)
        Zachary (Grandson)
    Kenneth (Kenny) - Married Jill Teodoro

APPENDIX B: A List of Memories

Basket picnics at Sugar Camp
Trips to Kennywood Park
Pony Rides at Kennywood Park
Riding the number 55 streetcar to Braddock
Riding the number 87 Ardmore streetcar to Pittsburgh
Streetcar tokens were 3 for 25 cents
Hot Dogs and Root Beer at the counter in Woolworth's 5 & 10
Skyscraper ice cream cones at Isaly's for 12 cents (my favorite was grape)
White Tower hamburgers
Postal stamps were 3 cents
Milk was 12 cents a quart
Funnel Cakes at Kennywood Park
Lunch cakes were 5 cents, Lunch pies were 6 cents
Candy Bars were 5 cents, Jumbo Candy Bars were 10 cents
Fresh Fish was 29 cents a pound
Cheese was 25 cents a pound
Bread was 6 cents for a regular size loaf, Large loaf was 12 cents
Hot Dogs were sold in a long string
Sawdust on the floor of Liberty Market and Ferri's Market
Sauerkraut bought from a barrel
Shopping at that wonderful G.C. Murphy's 5 & 10 store
Coney Island Hot Dogs
Aunt Irene taking us for long walks
Picking wildflowers
The smell of freshly mown grass
Resole kits for shoes that came with a cut-to-fit sole, scraper, and glue
Penny Candy
The candy counter at G.C. Murphy's 5 & 10
The "Suit Club" at Fineman's
The Saturday Matinee
Penn Cash Meat Market
Fresh meat wrapped in butcher's paper, tied up with string
Grummet's Variety Store

Crossing the foot bridge over the creek, near Taylor's Men's Store
The Jewel Tea Man
Watkins Pie Fillings
Mother's Hamilton Beach Mixer
The Flour Bin
The transom above the kitchen door
Clark Candy Bars
Fels-Naptha soap
Christmas lights on a circular series wire
The Westinghouse Store
Buying "live" poultry
Using a thimble when sewing
Hand washing laundry on a washboard
Reading my Nancy Drew books
Playing Hop-Scotch on the sidewalk
Catching lightening bugs in a glass jar
Collecting water in a rain barrel for watering plants
Playing catch in the field beyond the pear tree
Carving Halloween pumpkins
The Fuller Brush Man
Weeding the rose garden
Playing with Regina, Trudy, Rita, Marion, Dolly, & my other cousins
Swinging on the porch swing
My Father's smoking stand
Watching the parades in Turtle Creek
Saint Colman's Lawn Fete
Using Argo Starch
Sleeping with a feather tic cover at my Grandmother's house
The playground at the Electric Plan School
Bobbing for apples
Making snow angels
Snuggling up in bed with Irene, during the cold winter
Aunt Edna playing the violin
Getting books from the school library
My Mickey Mouse wristwatch
Aunt Dorothy doing my hair
Playing in the basement with Irene
Aunt Mary Figulski's delicious home-made bread
Cleaning the metal springs on the beds
Wallpaper cleaner
Playing with my paper dolls

Stringing popcorn at Christmas for the trees outdoors
Bonfires
Dish Night at the movies
The magic of the 5 & 10 at Christmastime
Watching my Father put chains on the car for driving in snow
Starting a plant from a sweet potato
Grandmother's and Mother's pretty aprons
Women wearing "House-Dresses"
Lisle Stockings
Wearing a dust bonnet while house-cleaning
My beautiful Shirley Temple Doll
The wide wooden staircase in the old Electric Plan School
Pens and inkwells in our school desks
Learning the "Peterson Handwriting Method"
Christmas parties at the V.F.W.
Barn Dances out at Young's Corner
The heavy traffic on Penn Avenue on a Saturday night
Wearing a hat and gloves to church
Mrs. Hohmann delivering fresh fruit and produce
Scent from blossoms of wild crabapple and pear trees
Making potato candy
Miss Arnold, my Art teacher at the Electric Plan School
Mr. Keefer, my Music teacher at the Electric Plan School
The "new" sound of The Andrews Sisters
The beautiful colors of the Fall leaves along the "Indian Path"

APPENDIX C: Recipes

My Mother's Specialties

Helen Krzyzosiak's Krusciki
(Polish Love Knots)

Helen Krzyzosiak's Paczkis
(Polish Filled Doughnuts)

Helen Krzyzosiak's Krusciki
(Polish Love Knots)

4 Eggs, beaten
1 - (8oz.) Sour Cream
Dash of Salt
1 teaspoon Nutmeg
1 cup Sugar
4 teaspoons Baking Powder
4 cups of Flour
Powdered Sugar

Combine dry ingredients. Add eggs and sour cream. Knead dough well, until stiff adding more flour if necessary. Separate dough into portions. Roll out on a floured surface to about ¼ inch thickness. With sharp knife, cut dough into strips about 1 & ½ inches wide by 5 inches long. Cut slit in center of each about 1 inch long and bring the end through the center to form a knot. Fry in hot grease (350 degrees), until golden brown, turning them and frying for about a minute on each side. Drain and cool slightly on paper towels. While warm, coat generously with powdered sugar.

Enjoy!

Helen Krzyzosiak's Paczkis
(Polish Filled Doughnuts)

2 cups Milk
1 cake Yeast
1/2 cup Sugar
7 cups Flour (sifted)
1/2 cup Butter melted and cooled
4 Egg Yolks, plus 1 whole Egg (room temperature)
1 teaspoon Salt
½ teaspoon Vanilla
½ teaspoon Nutmeg
Oil for frying
Apricot, Lecvar, or Cherry filling or preserves

Scald milk and cool to lukewarm. Add yeast, stirring until dissolved. Add 2 cups of the flour. Beat until dough forms. Cover and let rise in a warm place for about one hour. Cream the sugar, eggs and salt, stirring into the yeast mixture. Add nutmeg and vanilla. Add cooled, melted butter and remaining flour. Knead well. Place in a lightly greased bowl, cover and place in a warm place until double in size, about 1 hour. Roll out on floured surface to about ½ inch thickness. Cut with circular, floured doughnut cutter or inverted water glass dipped in flour. Cover and let rise again until double in size, about 1 more hour. Deep fry doughnuts in hot oil at 370 degrees, turning until golden brown. Drain on paper towels. When slightly cooled, cut 1 inch slit in the side of each doughnut. Using a pastry bag, fill each doughnut with filling or preserves, then roll doughnut in granulated sugar while still warm.

Enjoy!

In Acknowledgement

I wish to express my deepest gratitude and thanks:

To Dorothy Lance Gray - (The Krzyzosiak Family Historian),
I wish to thank you not only for inspiring me to write down everything that I remember, but for furnishing me with information that makes my story factually correct. Exact dates and names of ships require much research and that is very much appreciated. Your kindness and support during the creation of this book will never be forgotten.

To Karen Wakimoto,
I wish to thank you for helping with the editing on my story and for your kindness, encouragement, and friendship. Your meticulous attention to detail and perfection is truly appreciated. Our friendship and the friendship of your dear Mother, Kozuye, are greatly treasured.

To my Granddaughter Aaronell,
I wish to thank you for all of your efforts and technical assistance during the final edit of this book. Your expertise in computer skills is very much appreciated. It is up to you to continue on with this story.

To My Children, Dear Family, and Friends,
I wish to thank you for creating a lifetime of beautiful, wonderful memories that create the beautiful tapestry of my life. I encourage all of us to continue to add to its richness and color by sharing many more beautiful moments together.

CPSIA information can be obtained at www.ICGtesting.com
Printed in the USA
BVOW01*1329210814

363537BV00002B/131/P